HOW TO WRITE GREAT ESSAYS

HOW TO WRITE GREAT ESSAYS

Lauren Starkey

NEW YORK

Library of Congress Cataloging-in-Publication Data:
Starkey, Lauren B., 1962–
    How to write great essays / Lauren Starkey. —1st ed.
        p. cm.
    ISBN 1-57685-521-X
    1. English language—Rhetoric—Problems, exercises, etc.
2. Essay—Authorship—Problems, exercises, etc. 3. Report
writing—Problems, exercises, etc.   I. Title.
PE1471.S83 2004
808'.042—dc22

                                    2004003384

Printed in the United States of America

9 8 7 6 5 4 3 2 1

First Edition

ISBN 1-57685-521-X

For more information or to place an order, contact LearningExpress at:
    55 Broadway
    8th Floor
    New York, NY 10006

  Or visit us at:
    www.learnatest.com

Contents

Introduction

n your preparations for college, you may find yourself facing a handful of high-stakes essays. Your college application requires at least one, and the SAT requires another. Depending upon the high school you attend, or the state you reside in, you may need to write an exit essay, or take the Regents Exam. This book includes specific strategies to help you write great essays, no matter which type you write.

In contrast to basic writing guides that contain plenty of information you don't need, *How to Write Great Essays* focuses on the topics most important to you now. You won't find a comprehensive guide to mechanics, but instead you will get short but thorough lessons on the most common errors made in grammar, spelling, usage, and how to prevent and correct these errors. Every chapter is designed to relate directly to your essay, giving you the knowledge and the know-how you need to succeed.

The book is divided into seven chapters, with the first five covering different aspects of the writing process:

Chapter 1 shows you how to organize your thoughts and ideas before you begin writing, with techniques such as freewriting, brainstorming, and outlining. You will even learn why it's important to read good writing while preparing your essay.

Chapter 2 is about saying exactly what you mean by avoiding ambiguous language, using modifiers, eliminating unnecessary words and phrases, and using the active voice whenever possible.

Chapter 3 examines word choice and how it can accurately convey your ideas. It explains the most common misused and confused words, denotation versus connotation, and inclusive language. Important advice about the use of spell checking software is also included.

Chapter 4 teaches the most common mechanical errors so you can eliminate them from your writing. Troublesome parts of speech, issues such as noun-verb agreement, and punctuation problems are explained.

Chapter 5 shows you how to revise, edit, and proofread your essay. You will find checklists to use during these processes, as well as tips from professional editors. The use of word-processing programs to help with editing is also covered.

The last three chapters of *How to Write Great Essays* will arm you with specific strategies for writing both timed (SAT, GED) and untimed (college application, exit) essays.

Chapter 6 covers issues such as long-range planning, prewriting, and understanding the topics. Tips on writing to your audience and striking a balance between formality and informality are also explained.

Chapter 7 shows you how to prepare for timed essays. Learn how to research your exam, how to familiarize yourself with possible topic choices, and how to budget your time during the writing process. The more you know before writing a timed essay, the less stress you will feel during the exam, and the better the writing you will be able to produce.

Chapter 8 includes sample prompts and essays. Commentary at the end of each essay explains its strengths and weaknesses. You will be able to see how a number of writers approached both timed and untimed essay topics, and learn even more about how you can write a great essay.

No other essay resource, either in print or online, gives you all of the information found in this book. Everything from prewriting and grammar, to finding and taking practice essay exams is here. We have done our homework. Now it's time to do yours. Preparations begin with reading *How to Write Great Essays*.

HOW TO WRITE GREAT ESSAYS

Organization

I n a mythic vision, writers sit for hours, scribbling furiously to get down the incredibly brilliant words that seem to pour from their brains. But "mythic" is the operative word; it's not the reality experienced by most writers. Whether you are writing an essay for the SAT, your college application, or a graduation requirement, forget about the mythic vision. Even many professional writers find their craft to be a challenge. Journalist and biographer Gene Fowler noted that "writing is easy; all you do is sit staring at a blank sheet of paper until the drops of blood form on your forehead." Essay writing is rarely that tortuous. But it is important to recognize that in order to do it well, you must commit yourself to a process. Writing a great essay doesn't happen in one sitting. (Even when you are being timed, as with the SAT, your goal is not to turn out a finished piece, but rather to show that you know how to begin one.)

When the clock is ticking, and you are faced with a blank sheet of paper, don't wait for inspiration to strike (sometimes it doesn't). While creativity and inspiration can play an important role in good essay writing, organization, discipline, and revision are critical. Whether you have to write an essay in class, during a test, or for any type of application, getting down to the business of writing means focusing on these three things. This chapter deals with organization. When you begin your essay with organization, you will have guidance and direction through the writing process, especially if you are in a timed situation. Organization lets you see how your many developing ideas fit within a framework, and clearly maps out any type of essay you are required to write.

Organization also benefits the reader. By following one of the organizational methods at the end of this chapter, you will guide your reader from your first to last sentence. He or she will be able to see how the various points you make in your essay work together and how they support your thesis. The direction and purpose you get from organization helps your reader to believe what you are saying, and to willingly follow your lead. Practice the prewriting and organizational techniques detailed in this chapter. Determine ahead of time which work well for you, especially if you are going into a timed writing situation. Making the effort to think through what you want to say, and finding the best way to say it, will significantly improve your essay.

PERFECT TIMING

Regardless of how much time you have to complete your essay, try to follow these guidelines. Spend:

$\frac{1}{4}$ of your time prewriting and organizing
$\frac{1}{2}$ of your time writing
$\frac{1}{4}$ of your time revising and editing

▶ PREWRITING

Prewriting is the critical first step in creating a successful essay. Whether you are handed a topic, must come up with one on your own, or writing under a time constraint, taking the time to focus and shape your thoughts will result in a better final product. The six prewriting strategies explained below may be used both to generate new ideas and to clarify those you already have. Some strategies are better suited to a longer writing process such as the college admissions essay, while others may be adapted for when you have just a short period of time to complete an essay, as with the SAT. Prewriting strategies can also be used effectively when you are faced with a number of possible essay topics and must determine which is the best vehicle to express your unique thoughts and experiences.

1. FREEWRITING

Freewriting is probably the best-known prewriting technique. It works well when you have some thoughts on a topic, but can't envision them as an essay. Freewriting also functions as a developmental tool, nurturing isolated ideas into an essay-worthy one. People who use this technique often surprise themselves with what comes out on paper. It is common to discover a thought or point you didn't realize you had.

Specifically, freewriting means spending a predetermined period of time writing non-stop, focusing on a specific topic. In fact, freewriting might better be called "flow writing," because the most important aspect to this prewriting technique is the flow, or momentum, that comes when you stay with it. It works best when you write in full sentences, but phrases are also effective. The key is to keep writing without regard for grammar, spelling, or worthiness of ideas. Your speed will help keep you from being able to edit or throw out any ideas.

KEYS TO SUCCESSFUL FREEWRITING

- ◆ Resist the temptation to look back at what you have written during the process.
- ◆ If you can't stay on topic, keep writing anything to maintain the flow.
- ◆ Do not censor yourself; your freewriting is not going to be seen by others, so commit every thought to paper.
- ◆ Follow your ideas wherever they lead you.
- ◆ When finished, read your freewriting with a highlighter, noting the most interesting and strongest ideas.
- ◆ Try the process again after you have focused your topic; more ideas may be generated.

2. BRAINSTORMING OR LISTING

Brainstorming is similar to freewriting in that it is a timed, flowing exercise meant to elicit many thoughts and ideas on a given topic. However, instead of putting whole sentences or phrases to paper, this prewriting technique involves creating a list. It might contain various individual thoughts or ideas that make sense in a particular order, and/or ideas that are linked together by association with previous ideas. Unlike freewriting, brainstorming works well in a limited amount of time. Even with the twenty-five minutes allotted for the SAT essay, it is worthwhile to spend a few moments jotting down your ideas before beginning to write. Putting your ideas on paper will be especially helpful on the SAT, where your goal is to establish a point of view on a topic and support your position.

HOW TO BRAINSTORM

- ◆ If you are not already being timed, set a timer for at least five minutes (the more time you spend, the more and better ideas you will probably come up with).
- ◆ List every word or phrase that comes to mind about your topic. If you have not selected a topic, write in answers to the questions, "What do I have to say to my audience?" or "What do I want my audience to know about me?"

◆ As with freewriting, do not edit or censor any ideas, and ignore the rules of spelling, grammar, and punctuation.

◆ When you are finished, look over the list carefully. Cross out useless information and organize what is left. Categorize similar items.

3. CONCEPT MAPPING/ WEBBING

Mapping and webbing are graphic (visual) organizers that allow you to investigate the relationships between a number of diverse ideas. Concept mapping is a simple process best used for exploring topics that are not complex. To make one, draw a circle, and add spokes radiating from it. Put your central idea or subject in the middle, and add subtopics or related ideas around it in any order. Or, draw a box with your subject written in it, and continue adding boxes, connected to each other by arrows, showing the development of your idea. As with other prewriting techniques, do not judge yourself during this process. Write down any and every thought you have on your subject.

SAMPLE CONCEPT MAP

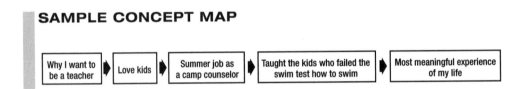

Why I want to be a teacher ▶ Love kids ▶ Summer job as a camp counselor ▶ Taught the kids who failed the swim test how to swim ▶ Most meaningful experience of my life

Creating a web takes more time, but may result in a more useful product. It works well when exploring a complex subject. To develop a web, write your topic in a circle. Next, write subtopics in smaller, or secondary circles, each connected to the center by a line. From each of the secondary circles, draw smaller bubbles in which you brainstorm possible solutions. Each possible solution is connected to the corresponding secondary bubble by a line.

Both maps and webs should be revised and reworked a number of times. When your ideas are on paper in one of these graphic organizers, it is easy to see how better to prioritize and organize them. Use maps and webs as flexible frameworks in which information may be moved around until it is in the correct place.

SAMPLE WEB

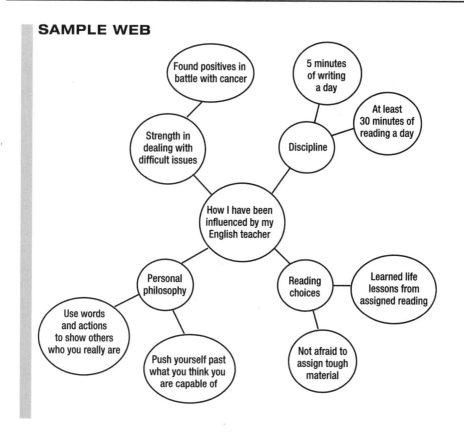

5. TAKING STOCK WITH THE 5 WS

Asking "who, what, where, when, and why" is a formula used by journalists, detectives, and researchers for getting a complete story. This technique is particularly useful for choosing an essay topic, and for focusing a topic once you have made a selection. There are two sets of questions for taking stock; one suited for an impersonal or research-type essay, and the other geared toward a personal essay. Unlike some of the other prewriting techniques, taking stock should be done deliberately, with great thought given to each question. Do not rush or include every idea that comes to mind. Even if you are being timed, take a moment to give the best answer you can for each question. The better focused your answers are, the more information you will have to use in your essay.

If you are writing a research paper or other type of non-personal writing, and your topic is already selected or assigned, concentrate on the standard W's: Who, What, Where, When, and Why. These questions will help you to quickly develop a great deal of information about your subject. Every question won't apply to every essay, and the prompts that follow each W are meant to be taken as suggestions. Be flexible and use the format as it best fits your topic.

1. **Who:** Who is involved? At what level? Who is affected?
2. **What:** What is your topic? What is its significance? What is at stake? What are the issues?

3. **Where:** Where does your subject occur? Where is its source?

4. **When:** When does your topic occur? When did it begin/end? When must action be taken to deal with it?

5. **Why:** Why is it our subject of interest? Why did it develop as it did? Why should others be interested in your topic?

Admissions essays and some exit essays are intended to be personal, so you must focus on yourself. Take time answering the personal, taking-stock questions below. This process involves a different set of W's, meant to elicit key information about yourself and about the topic if it has been chosen.

1. Where have you been (chronological history)?

2. What have you accomplished or achieved?

3. What do you do with your time when not in school?

4. What are you good at? What are you passionate about?

5. Who are/were your major influences?

6. READING GOOD WRITING

Consider your print diet: what are you reading in your spare time? This is an important question because what you read can influence what you write. The computer science term "garbage in, garbage out" applies. If you are reading mediocre writing, it won't help your essay, but if you consistently read great writing, it can make a difference with your own. Syntax, structure, and style can improve under the influence of writers who are masters at their craft.

The following list is based on suggestions made by English professors and teachers, college counselors, and admissions officers. It includes books and periodicals that cover current events, book reviews, science, history, race relations, sports, and other topics. Choose essays that appeal to you; there is no need to force yourself to read about something you are not interested in.

PERIODICALS

◆ *Harper's* (weekly magazine): essays, fiction, and reporting on political, literary, cultural, and scientific affairs.

◆ *The Economist* (daily newspaper): London publication covering world news, finance and economics, science and technology, books and arts, and business news.

◆ *The New Yorker* (weekly magazine): political and business reporting, social commentary, fiction, humor, art, poetry, and criticism.

BOOKS

◆ *The Art of the Personal Essay: An Anthology for the Classical Era to the Present*, Philip Lopate, editor (Anchor, 1997): over 75 essays written in the past 400 years by writers around the globe.

◆ *The Best American Essays 2003*, Robert Atwan and Anne Fadiman, editors (Mariner Books, 2003): annual publication since 1986—any year is fine; all volumes include a wide range of subjects.

◆ *The Best American Magazine Writing of 2003*, American Society of Magazine Editors, editors (Perennial, 2003): includes pieces on science, sports, current events, personalities, and fiction.

◆ *The Best American Science Writing*, Oliver Sacks, editor (Ecco, 2003): 25 essays on subjects representing most of the sciences, originally published in wide- and small-circulation periodicals.

▶ ORGANIZATION METHODS

With the exception of concept mapping and webbing, prewriting notes need organization before the writing of a first draft. There are many effective ways to organize your material before you start your first draft, so don't get hung up trying to find the one right way. Some people like outlines, both creating them and working from them. Others find them ineffective and should look at different techniques for imposing a scheme onto their prewriting notes.

OUTLINE

Creating an outline begins with a reading of your prewriting notes. First, group related ideas together, looking for major topics (which can be headings) and minor ones (which can be subheadings, examples, or details). Define your major points, and rearrange them until they make sense and follow a logical progression. You will be able to see the relationships between your ideas as you outline them, and determine their importance (major point, minor point, example, detail). If you need more supporting details or facts—subcategories—you can add them now. As you outline your information, use one-word topics, short phrases, or write out full sentences for each point on your outline.

If your prewriting notes are somewhat organized, you can use the outlining feature included in most word-processing programs to create an outline. Otherwise, arrange them yourself in a standard outline form using Roman and Arabic numerals and upper and lower case letters:

I.

   A.

   B.

      1.

      2.

         a.

         b.

Once you have completed an outline, revise and refine it by following these steps:

1. Write down your overall goal for your essay. What are you trying to say to your readers?
2. Go over your outline and circle, underline, or highlight your major points or images. Do they all support your goal?
3. Brainstorm words and phrases that will accurately and concisely express those points (jot them down in the margin of your outline, or use a separate sheet of paper).
4. Use this list and your outline to guide your writing. Do not allow yourself to stray from your goal or your major points.

PYRAMID CHARTS

As you reread your prewriting notes, answer the following:

- What is the purpose of my essay as a whole?
- What are the major parts of the whole, and how can they be categorized?
- What are the minor parts of the whole, and how do they relate to the major parts?
- What details can I use to illuminate both major and minor parts?

The answer to the first question is your thesis. Place it at the top of the pyramid. Below it, write the major parts and join them to the thesis with lines. Next, write the minor parts beneath the major ones, connecting them with lines. Finally, your details should be added under the parts to which they correspond.

SAMPLE PYRAMID CHART

Here is an example of a prewriting list and a corresponding pyramid chart.

Local school boards should not be allowed to ban books.

Freedom to read is guaranteed by the U.S. Constitution (1st amendment).

Give students credit—we don't believe everything we read.

Let us read books and decide what is right.

We need to learn how to think for ourselves.

Library Bill of Rights prohibits banning of books.

Parents and others should trust that we can read conflicting viewpoints and still hold our own values.

Censorship is wrong.

Education is about opening minds, and censorship is about closing them.

LIST

If you are having trouble with the highly structured outline or pyramid, try listing. Picture someone reading your completed essay. They will not see the framework behind your words, but instead will encounter each word, and thus each idea, one at a time. In other words, reading happens sequentially. With that in mind, organize your notes into a list based on one of the following strategies:

1. *Order of Importance:* rank supporting ideas from most important to least important, or vice versa.

2. *Chronological:* organize your ideas in the order in which they did happen or will happen.

3. *List:* create a roster of items of equal importance.
4. *General to Specific:* state supporting details, then the main point, or vice versa.

▶ FOR YOUR REVIEW

- Remember to use a variety of prewriting techniques, including freewriting, brainstorming, webbing, and concept mapping.
- Try different organizational methods such as outlines, pyramid charts, and lists.
- Don't forget that what you read affects your writing, so make sure you read the very best!

Clarity

After you submit it, your essay will be one in a large stack given to a reader or readers. In the case of college admissions, readers will have so many essays to read that they will spend only a few minutes on each. Exit and SAT essays will receive somewhat more time and attention, but it still holds that one reader will be responsible for a large number of essays. That is why it is imperative that you not only impress your reader(s) with your unique take on a topic, but also say exactly what you mean as clearly and, in many cases, as concisely as you can.

Your essay goal is to convey information, including the fact that you can write well. That goal won't be achieved if your readers don't understand your first few sentences or paragraphs, and stop reading, or if they finish reading but fail to grasp your message. Learning how to be a clear and accurate writer will help make your essay readable, and will guarantee that those who read it understand exactly what you mean to say. The five guidelines in this chapter show you how to clarify your writing.

▶ ELIMINATE AMBIGUITY

Ambiguous means having two or more possible meanings. Ambiguous language can either be words and phrases that have more than one meaning, or word order that conveys a meaning different from the one intended by the writer.

Example: *The quarterback liked to tackle his problems.*

This sentence can be read two ways: the quarterback likes to *deal with* his problems, or his problems are his opponents on the field whom he *grabs and knocks down*. This kind of confusion can happen whenever a word has more than one possible meaning. *The quarterback liked to address his problems* is a better sentence, and is unlikely to be misunderstood.

Example: *My advisor proofread my essay with the red sports car.*

Here, the *word order* of the sentence, not an individual word, causes the confusion. Did the advisor proofread the essay with his car? Because the phrase *with the red sports car* is in the wrong place, the meaning of the sentence is unclear. Try instead: *My advisor with the red sports car proofread my essay.*

CORRECTING AMBIGUOUS LANGUAGE

Ambiguous: *When doing the laundry, the phone rang.*
Clear: The phone rang when *I* was doing the laundry.

Ambiguous: *She almost waited an hour for her friend.*
Clear: She waited almost an hour for her friend.

Ambiguous: *I told her I'd give her a ring tomorrow.*
Clear: I told her I'd call her tomorrow.

Ambiguous: *A speeding motorist hit a student who was jogging through the park in her blue sedan.*
Clear: A speeding motorist in a blue sedan hit a student who was jogging through the park.

► MODIFIERS ADD PRECISION

Clarity in essay writing also involves the thoughtful use of modifiers, which make your point clear and add meaning and originality to your piece. One way to accomplish this is to use powerful and specific adjectives and adverbs. Consider the difference between these sets of sentences:

Sentence A: *My grandmother put on her sweater.*
Sentence B: *My grandmother put on her cashmere sweater.*

Sentence A: *The football team practiced in the rain.*
Sentence B: *The football team practiced in the torrential downpour.*

In both cases, sentence B allows you to hear the "voice" and impressions of the writer, giving a more accurate and interesting picture of the action. The first sentences are dull, and don't give the reader much information.

The right modifiers (adjectives and adverbs) can also get your message across in fewer, more accurate words. This is critical in an essay with a specified length. You don't want to sacrifice unique details, but sometimes one word will do the job better than a few. For example, *Chihuahua* can take the place of *little dog; exhausted* can take the place of *really tired;* and *late* can take the place of *somewhat behind schedule.*

MODIFIERS *QUALIFY* AND *QUANTIFY*

Qualify means to modify or restrict. In this sentence, words that qualify are in *italics*:
I am applying for a *civil engineering* internship with the *New York State* Department of Transportation.
Quantify means to express in numbers or measurement elements such as when, how much, how many, how often, and what scope. In this sentence, words that quantify are in *italics*:
For over *three years,* I have been a volunteer, delivering meals *four times* a week to over *twenty* people.

► POWERFUL, PRECISE ADJECTIVES AND ADVERBS

- unconditionally accepted
- forbidding alley
- unflagging dedication
- aimlessly walking

- grueling game
- mournful cry
- threadbare clothing
- invaluable lesson

Another technique for precise writing is pinpointing. Why leave your reader guessing, when you can tell him or her exactly what you mean? When you pinpoint, you replace vague words and phrases with specific ones. Consider the following sentence:

The character of Scrooge in Dicken's A Christmas Carol *is miserable.*

What does the writer mean by "miserable"? This is a vague word that conveys little meaning. A better sentence would use precise examples from the story to show what the writer means. For instance:

The character of Scrooge in Dicken's A Christmas Carol *is so miserly that he not only refuses comfortable surroundings for himself, but he also forces his employees to work long hours in a poorly heated room all winter.*

VAGUE AND SPECIFIC SENTENCES

Here are some sentences that lack accuracy, followed by better versions that use pinpointing:

Vague: *Janus needs to file his application soon.*
Specific: *Janus needs to file his application by January 4.*

Vague: *Space exploration has helped human beings in many ways.*
Specific: *The many benefits of space travel include the invention of fire detectors, calculators, Kevlar, and CATscan and MRI technologies.*

Vague: *Investing money in the stock market can be risky.*
Specific: *Over the last year, a $1,000 investment in a large-cap stock fund became worth $820. That same investment placed in a savings account totaled $1,065.*

Vague: *The new teacher is good.*
Specific: *The new teacher won "Teacher of the Year" awards six times at her previous school and has received federal grants for three student-led projects.*

► BE CONCISE

You won't score points with your readers by using five sentences that express an idea that could have been stated in one. Wordiness is boring, and it takes up valuable time and space. You have just 25 minutes to write the SAT essay, and most application essays are limited to 500 words, or two pages. That means you don't have the time or space to waste words. There are two equally important approaches to more concise writing: eliminating unnecessary words and phrases, and using the active (as opposed to passive) voice whenever possible. (For more information on the topic of active versus passive voice, including other reasons why you should avoid it, read through Chapter 4.)

Many of the words and phrases listed below are both well-known and, unfortunately, well-used. They don't convey meaning, and are therefore unnecessary. The following are three of the worst offenders, with usage examples.

1. *Because of the fact that.* In most cases, just *because* will do.
   Because of the fact that he was late, he missed his flight.
   Because he was late, he missed his flight.
2. *That* and *which* phrases. Eliminate them by turning the idea in the *that* or *which* phrase into an adjective.
   These were directions that were well-written.
   These directions were well-written.
3. *That* by itself is a word that often clutters sentences unnecessarily, as in the following examples:
   The newscaster said that there was a good chance that election turnout would be low and that it could result in a defeat for our candidate.
   The newscaster said there was a good chance election turnout would be low and it could result in a defeat for our candidate.

WORD CHOICES FOR CONCISE WRITING

Wordy	Replace with
a lot of	*many* or *much*
all of a sudden	*suddenly*
along the lines of	*like*
are able to	*can*
as a matter of fact	*in fact* or Delete
as a person	Delete
as a whole	Delete
as the case may be	Delete
at the present time	*currently* or *now*
both of these	*both*

by and large	Delete
by definition	Delete
due to the fact that	*because*
for all intents and purposes	Delete
has a tendency to	*often* or Delete
has the ability to	*can*
in order to	*to*
in the event that	*if*
in the near future	*soon*
is able to	*can*
it is clear that	Delete
last but not least	*finally*
on a daily basis	*daily*
on account of the fact that	*because*
particular	Delete
somewhere in the neighborhood of	*about*
take action	*act*
the fact that	*that* or Delete
the majority of	*most*
the reason why	*the reason* or *why*
through the use of	*through*
with regard to	*about* or *regarding*
with the exception of	*except for*

▶ WORDY AND CONCISE SENTENCES

Wordy: The students were given detention on account of the fact that they didn't show up for class.
Concise: The students were given detention because they didn't show up for class.

Wordy: Everyone who has the ability to donate time to a charity should do so.
Concise: Everyone who can donate time to a charity should.

Wordy: In a situation in which a replacement for the guidance counselor who is retiring is found, it is important that our student committee be notified.
Concise: When a replacement for the retiring guidance counselor is found, our student committee must be notified.

► AVOID UNNECESSARY REPETITION

There are a number of reasons why you should eliminate the repetition of ideas and information in your essay. The first is that unnecessary repetition is a sign of sloppy writing. It's easy to say the same thing a number of times, varying it slightly each time. It's harder to say something well once, and continue writing about your next idea or example. Second, wordiness wastes valuable time and space. If you are writing while the clock is ticking, or are limited to a number of words or pages, say it right the first time and move on.

> **Example:**
> **Wordy:** They met at 4 P.M. in the afternoon.
> **Concise:** They met at 4 P.M.

P.M. means in the afternoon, so there's no reason to say *in the afternoon*. It's a waste of words and the reader's time.

Even in short phrases there can be repetition. The list that follows contains dozens of such phrases that can clutter your essay. Most of them contain a specific word and its more general category. But why state both? The word "memories" can only refer to the past, so you don't need to say "past memories." We know that blue is a color, so describing something as "blue in color" is repetitive and therefore unnecessary. In most cases, you can correct the redundant phrase by dropping the category and retaining the specific word.

Some of the phrases use a modifier that is unneeded, because the specific is implied in the general. For instance, the word "consensus" means general agreement. Therefore, modifying it with the word "general" is repetitive. Similarly, "mathematics" is a field of study, so it does not need to be modified with the word "field." You can tighten up your writing, saying it well one time, by eliminating wordiness.

> **TRY THIS!**
>
> As you read the list, jot down those you know you use on a separate sheet of paper. Write next to each phrase on your list the correction of that phrase, along with a couple of sentences using it correctly. This technique will help you retain the information better.

Retain only the first word:

any and all	heavy in weight	confused state
first and foremost	period in time	modern in design
refer back	round in shape	unusual in nature
close proximity	odd in appearance	extreme in degree
large in size	mathematics field	strange type
often times	cheap quality	
reason why	honest in character	

Drop the modifier (first word):

past memories	true facts	free gift
final destination	important essentials	past history
general consensus	future plans	totally obvious
various differences	terrible tragedy	rarely ever
each individual	end result	unexpected surprise
basic fundamentals	final outcome	sudden crisis

▶ USE PRONOUNS CAREFULLY

Pronouns (words such as *I*, *we*, *them*, and *her*) take the place of nouns. They should only be used when the noun to which they refer (known as the *antecedent*) is obvious and meaningful. Check the pronouns in your writing to be certain they are not one of the following:

- unclear
- too far from the antecedent
- useless

Example: *Trini is interested in teaching and farming, which is her career choice.*

What is her career choice? *Which* could mean either teaching or farming, making it unclear. The writer needs to restate the career instead of using a pronoun in order to eliminate the possibility the reader will not understand the sentence. Write instead: *Trini is interested in teaching and farming, but farming is her career choice.*

Example: *Bring the paper with you tomorrow to the meeting that discusses the detention policy.*

The pronoun *that* is too far away from its antecedent to be clear. It could refer to the paper, or to the meeting. A better sentence is: *Bring the paper that discusses the detention policy with you to the meeting tomorrow.*

Example: *They always talk about the dangers of global warming.*

This common pronoun error is also known as an expletive: *they* is useless, because it appears to refer to no one. If the writer has that information, he or she can revise the sentence to be more precise: *The newspaper frequently has articles about the dangers of global warming.* If there is truly no *they,* the sentence should be revised by eliminating it: *There is much talk about the dangers of global warming.*

MORE EXAMPLES PRONOUN USAGE

Incorrect: Both Fellini and Bergman edited *his* movie.
Correct: Both Fellini and Berman edited *Bergman's* movie.

Incorrect: Leave all ingredients out of the recipes *that do not belong* in a healthy diet.
Correct: Leave all ingredients *that do not belong* in a healthy diet out of the recipes.

Incorrect: *They* banned parking in their lot so the snowplows could do their job.
Correct: *The owners of the parking lot* banned parking in their lot so the snowplows could do their job.

Incorrect: The Civil War and the Spanish American War took place in the nineteenth century. It was a turning point for the country.
Correct: The Civil War and the Spanish American War took place in the nineteenth century. The Civil War was a turning point for the country.

▶ FOR YOUR REVIEW

- Avoid ambiguous language by staying away from words and phrases that have more than one meaning, and correcting word order that conveys a meaning different from the one intended.
- Use modifiers, such as powerful and specific adjectives and adverbs, to clarify your writing. Replace vague words and phrases with ones that are specific.
- Be concise by eliminating unnecessary words and phrases, and using the active (as opposed to passive) voice whenever possible.

- Don't repeat ideas or information in your essay; it is a sign of sloppy writing and wastes valuable time and space.
- Pronouns should be used when the antecedent is obvious and meaningful.

Word Choice

One of the best ways to accurately convey your ideas in your essay is to choose the right words. Doing so ensures that your audience understands what you are writing. Also, with the exception of essays on national exams such as the SAT or GED, spelling counts. In fact, it is critical that your essay be mistake-free. If you are typing your essay, you can use the spell check feature, but don't rely on it alone. Knowledge of basic spelling rules will help you to craft an essay that gives your reader a positive impression. To learn about these topics, keep reading.

This sounds simple, and for the most part, it is. You already have a command of the English language that includes knowledge of the denotative (literal) meaning of thousands of words. Therefore, all you need to do is choose the right ones to get your message across. The first section of this chapter explains some of the pitfalls of word choice, including commonly confused and misused words.

However, saying what you mean takes more than just an understanding of the **denotation**, or literal meaning, of a word. Many words also have a connotative meaning. The **connotation** is a word's implied meaning, which involves emotions, cultural assumptions, and suggestions. Both meanings must be considered when making word choices.

Once you recognize denotative and connotative meaning, you must consider whether the words you choose might confuse or possibly offend your audience. That means being aware of inclusive language, and avoiding slang, clichés, and buzzwords. Your essay is an important opportunity to get a positive message across. Don't miss it by inadvertently insulting, confusing, or annoying your reader.

▶ DENOTATION

The words in this section are frequently used incorrectly. The confusion may stem from words that sound or look similar (but have very different meanings), words and usages that sound correct (but in fact are not considered standard English), or words that are misused so often that their wrong usage is thought to be correct. When you are unsure of the denotation, or dictionary meaning, of a word, you are more likely to make these kinds of mistakes. As you read this section, make a note of any words you think you have used incorrectly. Read the definitions carefully, and be certain that you understand proper usage before moving on.

MISTAKEN IDENTITY

When you use the wrong words, your writing suffers. One incorrect choice—using *illicit* when you mean *elicit*, for example—can completely change the meaning of a sentence. Because there are many English words that sound or look almost identical, but have very different meanings, choosing the right one can be difficult. You must understand the correct meaning of the words you use in order to avoid "mistaken identity."

The following list of the most commonly confused words can improve your writing by showing you how to avoid such errors. As you read it, take note of those you have used incorrectly. You may want to write them down, along with a couple of sentences in which you use them correctly. In your essay writing, pay careful attention to the denotative meaning of every word you use.

Confused Words	Definition
a lot (noun):	many
allot (verb):	to give or share in arbitrary amounts
accept (verb):	to recognize
except (prep.):	excluding
access (noun, verb):	means of approaching; to approach
excess (noun, adj.):	extra
addition (noun):	increase
edition (noun):	an issue of a book or newspaper

advice (noun):	a recommended opinion
advise (verb):	to give advice; inform
affect (verb):	to influence
effect (noun):	result
effect (verb):	to bring about
all ready (adj.):	completely prepared
already (adv.):	by or before a specified or implied time
all together (adj.):	in a group; in unison
altogether (adv.):	completely or thoroughly
allude (verb):	to refer to something not specifically mentioned
elude (verb):	to escape notice or detection
ascent (noun):	the act of climbing or rising
assent (verb):	to agree or accept a proposal or opinion
assure (verb):	to make certain (assure someone)
ensure (verb):	to make certain
insure (verb):	to secure from harm; to secure life or property in case of loss
beside (adj.):	next to
besides (adv.):	in addition to
bibliography (noun):	list of writings
biography (noun):	a life story
capital (noun):	money invested; a town or city where the government sits
capitol (noun):	a government building
choose (verb):	to select
chose (verb):	the past tense of choose
cite (verb):	to acknowledge; to quote as a reference
sight (noun):	the ability to see; vision
site (noun):	a place or location

complement (noun):	match
compliment (noun, verb):	praise; to give praise
consul (noun):	an official appointed by the government to live in a foreign city and attend to the interests of the official's country
council (noun):	a group of people called together to provide advice
counsel (noun, verb):	advice; to give advice
continual (adj.):	taking place in close succession
continuous (adj.):	without break or let up
cooperation (noun):	assistance, help
corporation (noun):	type of business organization
decent (adj.):	well-mannered
descent (noun):	decline, fall
dissent (noun):	disagreement
desert (noun):	arid, sandy region
dessert (noun):	sweet served after a meal
disburse (verb):	to pay
disperse (verb):	to spread out
disinterested (adj.):	no strong opinion either way
uninterested (adj.):	don't care
elicit (verb):	to stir up
illicit (adj.):	illegal
envelop (verb):	to surround; to cover completely
envelope (noun):	flat paper container for letters or other documents
farther (adv.):	beyond
further (adj.):	additional

flack (noun, verb):	press agent (noun); to act as a press agent (verb)
flak (noun):	criticism
forth (adv.):	forward, onward
fourth (adj.):	next in number after the third
hear (verb):	to perceive by the ear
here (adv.):	in this or at this place
hoard (verb):	to collect and keep
horde (noun):	a huge crowd
imply (verb):	to hint or suggest
infer (verb):	to assume, deduce
loose (adj.):	not restrained, not fastened
lose (verb):	to fail to win; be deprived of
loath (adj.):	reluctant
loathe (verb):	to feel hatred for
medal (noun):	a badge of honor
meddle (verb):	to interfere
metal (noun):	a mineral substance
passed (verb):	the past tense of past
past (adj.):	finished; gone by
personal (adj.):	individual
personnel (noun):	employees
principal (adj.):	main
principal (noun):	person in charge
principle (noun):	standard
quiet (adj.):	still; calm
quit (verb):	to stop; to discontinue
quite (adv.):	very; fairly; positively

stationary (adj.):	not moving
stationery (noun):	writing paper
taught (verb):	the past tense of teach
taut (adj.):	tight
than (conj., prep.):	in contrast to
then (adv.):	next
their (pronoun):	belonging to them
there (adv.):	in a place
they're:	contraction for *they are*
to (prep.):	in the direction of
too (adv.):	also; excessively
two (adj.):	the number after one
weather (noun, verb):	atmospheric conditions; to last or ride out
whether (conj.):	if it be the case; in either case
who (pronoun):	substitute for he, she, or they
whom (pronoun):	substitute for him, her, or them
your (pronoun):	belonging to you
you're:	contraction for *you are*

HOMONYMS

When you look back over the list above, note how many word pairs or groups sound the same, or nearly the same. However, their spellings and meanings are very different. Many of them are also different parts of speech (such as *elicit*, which is a verb, and *illicit*, which is an adjective). These pairs or groups are known as *homonyms*, and they sometimes confuse even professional writers. The secret to avoiding errors with homonyms is to understand their exact meaning. When you are certain of a word's denotation, you will use it correctly, and won't confuse it with another, similar-sounding, word.

MISUSED NO LONGER

Along with confused words, add commonly misused words to the list of poor word choices. These words are used incorrectly in the media, on billboards and other signs, in speech, and in writing every day. In fact, probably because the errors are so common, they often sound acceptable to many people. But to good writers and the readers of your essay, they are glaring errors. Take the time to learn the denotative meanings of the most commonly misused words to ensure proper usage.

Word	**When to Use It**
allude:	used when a reference is made indirectly or covertly
refer:	used when something is named or otherwise mentioned directly
amount:	used when you cannot count the items to which you are referring, and when referring to singular nouns
number:	used when you can count the items to which you are referring, and when referring to plural nouns
anxious:	nervous
eager:	enthusiastic, or looking forward to something
among:	used when comparing or referring to three or more people or things
between:	used for two people or things
bring:	moving something toward the speaker
take:	moving something away from the speaker

> **Hint:** Remember, bring *to*, take *away*

can:	used to state ability
may:	used to state permission
each other:	when referring to two people or things
one another:	when referring to three or more people or things
e.g.:	an abbreviation for the Latin *exempli gratia*, meaning *free example* or *for example*
i.e.:	an abbreviation for the Latin *id est*, meaning *it is* or *that is*

feel bad:	used when talking about physical ailments
feel badly:	used when talking about emotional distress
fewer:	when you can count the items
less:	when you cannot count the items
good:	an adjective, which describes a person, place, or thing
well:	an adverb, which describes an action or verb
its:	belonging to *it*
it's:	contraction of *it is*

Hint: Unlike most possessives, *it* doesn't have an apostrophe.

lay:	the action of placing or putting an item somewhere; a transitive verb, meaning something you do *to* something else
lie:	to recline or be placed (a lack of action); an intransitive verb, meaning it does not act on anything or anyone else
more:	used to compare one thing to another

Hint: one of the two can be a collective noun, such as *the ballplayers* or *the Americans.*

most:	used to compare one thing to more than one other thing
supposably:	capable of being supposed
supposedly:	believed to be the case
that:	a pronoun that introduces a restrictive (or essential) clause
which:	a pronoun that introduces a non-restrictive (or unessential) clause

Hint: Imagine a parenthetical *by the way* following the word *which*. "The book, which (by the way) Joanne prefers, is her first novel," is incorrect. Therefore, it should read "The book that Joanne prefers is her first novel." "Lou's pants, which (by the way) are black, are made of leather," is correct.

AVOID AT ALL COSTS

It doesn't matter how often they are used, the words (and usages) mentioned in this rule are not considered standard English and should never be used.

acrrosed/acrost: the adverb and preposition *across* has only one form; it never ends in the letter *t*

alot: incorrect spelling of *a lot;* often seen in informal writing, but should not be used in an essay or any other formal writing

alright: incorrect spelling of *all right*

anyways: speech dialect form not acceptable in written English; use *anyway*

anywheres: see *anyways*

arguably: considered vague and overused; often appears as a dangling modifier

brang/brung: often seen masquerading as the past tense of *bring; brought* is the only correct past tense of bring

conversate: an unacceptable back-formation of *conversation;* use *converse* instead

everywheres: see *anyways*

go: should not be used to report speech ("He goes, 'I quit.' ")

hopefully: most often heard as a substitute for "I hope;" as such it is not a word. "*Hopefully* I'll get an A on the test" is an example of nonstandard English. What the writer means is "I hope I'll get an A on the test." *Hopefully* is a word, however, when used as an adverb to mean full of hope. For example: They waited *hopefully* for the firefighters.

irregardless: this blend of irrespective and regardless has been in use for about a century, but is still not considered a word in standard written English

majorly/minorly: major and minor are adjectives; these substandard forms are attempts to use the words as adverbs. Other words, such as "somewhat," should be used instead.

nother: incorrect form of another

nowheres: see *anyways*

somewheres: see *anyways*

theirselves/themself: both are incorrect forms of *themselves;* because *them* is plural, *self* must be as well. Also, *their* combined with *selves* is incorrect because it suggests possession.

▶ CONNOTATION

When you are certain you have selected your words carefully, each one denoting exactly what you intend it to, you must then consider connotation. What shades of meaning are suggested? Think beyond the dictionary, or denotative meaning, to what might be implied or inferred by your writing.

POSITIVE AND NEGATIVE CONNOTATION

Connotation involves emotions, cultural assumptions, and suggestions. Connotative, or implied, meanings can be positive, negative, or neutral. Some dictionaries offer usage notes that help to explain connotative meanings, but they alone can't be relied on when trying to avoid offensive or incorrect word choices. Keep in mind that using a word without being aware of its implied meaning can annoy your reader or make your message unclear.

For example, what feelings come to mind when you hear the words *plagiarize* or *copy*? *Plagiarize* has negative connotations, while *copy* is a more neutral selection. *Blunder* or *oversight*? *Leer* or *look*?

If you were making travel plans, would you choose to rent a car from an agency whose safety record was described as *adequate*? Although the dictionary definition of the word is "sufficient" or "meeting a requirement," the connotative meaning is negative: "barely satisfactory." Consider all the meanings your words might reveal, and determine whether they belong in your writing.

Examples

Positive or Neutral Connotation	Negative Connotation
teenager	punk
knife	dagger
individualist	eccentric
youthful	childish
ethical	straight-laced
aggressive	pushy
thrifty	cheap
challenging	perplexing
homeless	vagrant
natural	plain
statesman	politician
smile	smirk
clever	sly

INCLUSIVE LANGUAGE

Biased language, which includes negative stereotypes, has no place in your writing. Your goal is to include rather than to exclude. Understanding the purpose of inclusive language, and using it in your essay, will assure that your message gets across without creating or perpetuating negative social stereotypes. Use the following techniques to help you to replace any possibly offensive words and phrases with inclusive language.

Gender

- Avoid the suffix *-ess,* which has the effect of minimizing the significance of the word to which it is attached (*actor* is preferable to *actress, proprietor* to *proprietress*).
- Do not overuse *he* and *him.* Instead, use *his* or *her* or *their* and *those*; or alternate between *him* and *her.*
- Degender titles. *Businessman* becomes *businessperson* or *executive, chairman* becomes *chair* or *chairperson, stewardess* becomes *flight attendant, weatherman* becomes *meteorologist.*
- When referring to a couple, don't make assumptions. *Inappropriate*: Mr. Rosenberg and Caryn, Mr. and Mrs. Bill Rosenberg. *Appropriate*: Mr. Rosenberg and Ms. Fetzer
- Use professional, rather than personal, descriptive terms. *Inappropriate*: Robin Benoit, a lovely novelist. *Appropriate*: Robin Benoit, an experienced novelist.
- Avoid making assumptions about traditionally exclusive arenas such as the home and sports. Not all women are homemakers, and not all homemakers are women. The word *housewife* should not be used. Similarly, not all team members are male. *Sportsmanship* should be replaced with *fair play,* and *crewmen* should be *crew members.*

Race

- To avoid stereotyping, leave out any reference to race, unless it is relevant to the subject of your writing.
- Focus on a person's individual, professional characteristics and qualifications, not racial characteristics.

Disability

- Discuss the *person*, not their handicap.
- If your writing is specifically focused on disabilities or disease, or you must mention them for another reason, do not use words that imply victimization or create negative stereotypes. Terms such as *victim, sufferer, poor, afflicted,* and *unfortunate* should be omitted.

- Don't use *courageous* to describe a person with a disability unless the context allows the adjective to be used for all. Someone is not courageous because they are deaf, but they may be because they swam the English Channel.
- Always put the person ahead of the disability, as in *person with impaired hearing*, rather than *hearing-impaired person*.

▶ AVOID OVERLY INFORMAL AND OVERUSED LANGUAGE

Colloquialisms are words and phrases appropriate for speech and very informal or casual writing. They don't belong in your essay unless you are trying to imitate speech or assume a very informal tone for effect. Colloquialisms include vulgarisms (obscene or offensive words), clichés, and slang.

Your reader is not going to consult a dictionary to understand what you've written, nor will he or she be impressed with stale, highly unoriginal language. Eliminate any words or phrases that are overused, or that might be unfamiliar to your reader. A word or two in a foreign language, which you translate immediately, is ok. The use of confusing technical language or buzzwords is not.

- **Vulgarisms**—the last thing you want to do is turn off or offend your reader. Since you do not know your audience, you do not know exactly what kinds of language they may find offense or in poor taste. Err on the side of caution by not including any language considered even mildly obscene, gross, or otherwise offensive. This includes scatological and sexual terms, and words such as bitch (as in "life is a bitch"), hell (as in "hotter than hell"), God (as in "oh, God!"), and damn.
- **Clichés**—clichés should be avoided not only because they are too informal, but also because they are overused. Your essay must not rely on stale phrases such as: *one step at a time; no news is good news; don't worry, be happy; when life gives you lemons, make lemonade;* and *no guts, no glory.*
- **Slang**—slang is non-standard English. Its significance is typically far-removed from either a word's denotative or connotative meaning, and is particular to certain groups (therefore, it excludes some readers who won't understand it). Examples include: *blow off, canned, no sweat,* and *thumbs down (or up)*. It is also inappropriate and in poor taste to use slang terms for racial or religious groups.

► SPELLING

College admissions essays and essays that are not timed must not contain a single spelling error. Even if the errors are slight, they can add up to an impression that is decidedly against the one you are trying to convey. In fact, essay readers have described spelling mistakes as making the writer seem "sloppy," "unprofessional," "not as smart," "lazy," and even "foolish."

Putting in a little time will improve your spelling quickly. You can learn and use the following simple spelling rules that cover the few dozen mistakes which account for the majority of errors. These rules will help you no matter what type of essay you are writing, because once you know them, you can use them at any time. In addition, you can become a more proficient user of your computer's spell check feature. Last, give your essay to at least two good readers who will check for any spelling errors you may have missed.

BASIC SPELLING RULES—I BEFORE E

I before E except after C, or when sounding like A as in neighbor *or* weigh.

Though it has a few exceptions, this simple rule is worth remembering. The majority of the time, it works. Some examples of the exceptions:

> After C: *ceiling, conceive, deceive, perceive, receipt, receive, deceit, conceit*
> When sounding like A: *neighbor, freight, beige, sleigh, weight, vein, weigh*
> Others: *either, neither, feint, foreign, forfeit, height, leisure, weird, seize,* and
> *seizure*

BASIC SPELLING RULES—DOUBLING FINAL CONSONANTS

When adding an ending to a word that ends in a consonant, you double the consonant if:

- the ending begins with a vowel (such as *-ing, -ed, -age, -er, -ence, -ance,* and *-al*)
- the last syllable of the word is accented and that syllable ends in a single vowel followed by a single consonant (words with only one syllable are always accented). *Stop* becomes *stopping, stopped, stoppage,* or *stopper* because *stop* has only one syllable (so it is accented), and it ends in a single consonant preceded by a single vowel.

Here are some other examples of words that meet the doubling requirements:

> run—running, runner
> slam—slamming, slammed
> nag—nagged, nagging
> incur—incurred, incurring
> kid—kidding, kidder

plan—planned, planning, planner
begin—beginning, beginner
set—setting
transmit—transmitting, transmittal, transmitted

BASIC SPELLING RULES—DROPPING FINAL E'S AND Y'S

When adding an ending to a word that ends with a silent *e*, drop the final *e* if the ending begins with a vowel, such as *advancing* and *surprising*.

If the ending begins with a consonant, keep the final *e*, as in *advancement* and *likeness*.

However, if the silent *e* is preceded by another vowel, drop the *e* when adding any ending (*argument, argued, truly*).

EXCEPTIONS TO THE RULES

To avoid confusion and mispronunciation, the final *e* is kept in words such as *mileage* and words where the final *e* is preceded by a soft *g* or *c*: *changeable, courageous, manageable, management*, and *noticeable*. The word *management*, for example, would be pronounced with a hard *g* sound if not for the *e* after the *g*. If the root word ends with a silent *e*, and the suffix begins with a vowel, then take off the silent *e* and add the suffix.

come + ing = coming

If the root word ends with a consonant followed by the letter *y*, change the *y* to *i* and add the suffix.

reply + ed = replied

BASIC SPELLING RULES—PLURALS

Most words are made plural by simply adding an *s*. However, if a word ends in *x* or *s*, *-sh* or *-ch*, the suffix *-es* must be added to form a plural.

church/churches
box/boxes
plus/plusses

If the word ends in a consonant plus *-y*, change the *-y* into *-ie* and add an *-s* to form the plural.

enemy/enemies
baby/babies

When in doubt, look up the singular form in the dictionary, where you will also find the plural listed.

COMMONLY MISSPELLED WORDS

absence	dilemma	lieutenant	receive
abundance	discrepancy	lightning	recommend
accidentally	eighth	loophole	reference
accommodate	eligible	losing	referred
acknowledgment	embarrass	maintenance	regardless
acquaintance	equivalent	maneuver	relevant
aggravate	euphoria	mathematics	religious
alibi	existence	millennium	remembrance
alleged	exuberance	minuscule	reservoir
ambiguous	feasible	miscellaneous	responsible
analysis	February	misspell	restaurant
annual	fifth	negotiable	rhythm
argument	forcibly	ninth	ridiculous
awkward	forfeit	occasionally	roommate
basically	formerly	occurred	scary
boundary	fourth	omission	scissors
bulletin	fulfill	opportunity	secretary
calendar	grateful	outrageous	separate
canceled	grievance	pamphlet	souvenir
cannot	guarantee	parallel	specifically
cemetery	guidance	perceive	sufficient
coincidence	harass	permanent	supersede
committee	hindrance	perseverance	temperament
comparative	ideally	personnel	temperature
completely	implement	possess	truly
condemn	independence	potato	twelfth
congratulations	indispensable	precede	ubiquitous
conscientious	inoculate	preferred	unanimous
consistent	insufficient	prejudice	usually
convenient	interference	prevalent	usurp
correspondence	interrupt	privilege	vacuum
deceive	jealousy	procedure	vengeance
definitely	jewelry	proceed	visible
dependent	judgment	prominent	Wednesday
depot	leisure	pronunciation	wherever
descend	length	quandary	
desperate	lenient	questionnaire	
development	liaison	receipt	

▶ USING COMPUTER SPELL CHECKERS

There is no excuse for not using spell check. It's fast and simple, and catches many common spelling errors and typos. However, spell check is not fool-proof. As professional editor Deborah Wenger says, "use it, but dew knot rely on it exclusively." You should be aware of its three most important limitations and rely on other methods to catch possible errors, especially for more important documents.

1. *Non-Word versus Real-Word Errors*
   Most of us think of spelling errors in the first category, that is, a string of letters that does not make a real word. You might type *sevn* instead of *seven*, or *th* for *the*. Spell check is an excellent tool for catching these types of mistakes. However, if you are discussing the seven years of piano lessons you have taken, and you leave off the *s* and type *even*, spell check won't flag your error.

   This is known as a real word error. You have typed a legitimate, correctly spelled word; it's just not the word you meant to type, and it doesn't convey the meaning you intended. Spell check can't find these types of errors.

2. *Proper Nouns*
   Spell check uses a dictionary that does not include most proper nouns and words in other categories, such as the names of chemicals. You can always add a word or words to the dictionary once you are sure of its spelling, but the first time you spell check, you will need to use another source (a reliable print one is best) to verify the spelling.

3. *Errors Spelled Similarly to Another Real Word*
   If you misspell a word in such a way that it is now closer, letter-by-letter, to a word other than the one you intended, spell check will probably offer the wrong word as a correction. For example, if your essay includes a coffee house scenario, and you type the word *expresso*, spell check will correct the error with *express* rather than *espresso*. Similarly, *alot* will be "corrected" to *allot*. You must pay careful attention to spell check's suggested corrections to ensure the right selection.

▶ FOR YOUR REVIEW

- One of the best ways to accurately convey your ideas is to choose the right words. Doing so ensures that your audience understands the meaning you intend.
- Many words are confused because they sound or look almost identical, but have very different meanings.

- Take the time to learn the denotative meanings of the most commonly misused words to ensure proper usage.

- Some words and word usages appear frequently in print although they are not considered standard English. Avoid them in your writing.

- Choose words by keeping in mind their implied (connotative) as well as literal meanings. Their connotations involve emotions, cultural assumptions, and suggestions that can be positive, negative, or neutral.

- Understanding the purpose of inclusive language and using it in your essay, will assure that your message gets across without creating or perpetuating negative social stereotypes.

- Almost all of the most common spelling errors can be corrected by learning and applying four basic spelling rules.

- Always use a spell checker, but never rely on it completely.

Mechanics

The majority of grammar, punctuation, and capitalization mistakes are just a few dozen common ones. If you learn these common errors and how to avoid or correct them, your writing will greatly improve. Therefore, the focus of this chapter is on those errors that occur most frequently.

No matter how original an idea you come up with, the inability to express yourself clearly and accurately through the written word will hinder the success of your essay. The rules of mechanics are complex; in fact, they sometimes confuse even professional writers. However, you do not need to become a strict grammarian in order to write well.

▶ PARTS OF SPEECH

Some parts of speech are more difficult than others. Following are the four most challenging ones as they pertain to your essay: pronouns, adjectives, adverbs, and prepositions, with usage explanations and examples.

If you feel your writing would benefit from a more in-depth review of grammar, check the resources at the end of this book for websites and books that contain grammar lessons, practice exercises, and quizzes to reinforce the material.

PRONOUNS

Pronouns refer back to or take the place of nouns. They should:

1. **Agree in number**
    A singular pronoun must be used for a singular noun.
    Incorrect: If *the student* passes this course, *they* will graduate.
    Correct: If *the student* passes this course, *she* will graduate.

2. **Agree in person**
    Do not switch back and forth in your writing from the first person (*I*) to the second (*you*) or third (*he, she, they, it*).

    First person pronouns: *I, me, we, us*
    Second: *you*
    Third: *he, she, him, her, they, them*

    Incorrect: When *a person* comes to class, *you* should have your homework ready.
    Correct: When *a person* comes to class, *he* should have his homework ready.

3. **Be a specific reference to a noun**
    It should be obvious to your reader to which noun the pronoun refers.

    Incorrect: Kim spends all his time reading and playing soccer, but it isn't good for him.
    (What isn't good for him? Reading, playing soccer, or both?)
    Correct: Kim spends all his time reading and playing soccer. Too much soccer isn't good for him; he should play some basketball, too.

    Incorrect: It has been years since *they* spent money on new textbooks.
    Who is they?
    Correct: It has been years since the school board spent money on new textbooks.

    Incorrect: I went on the trip with Emily and Nancy, and we took her laptop.
    (Whose laptop?)
    Correct: I went on the trip with Emily and Nancy, and we took Nancy's laptop.

ADJECTIVES

Adjectives describe or modify nouns or pronouns. Adjectives add information by describing people, places, or things in a sentence. These words, more than any others, make your essay a unique piece. Use them to describe people, objects, and situations to make the reader understand your point of view and see things the way you have seen them. Too few adjectives will make a personal statement a boring play-by-play that doesn't tell the reader anything about the writer.

ADVERBS

Adverbs, which describe verbs, are easily spotted because most of them end in *-ly*, such as *slowly, quickly, abruptly*. However, the adverb that causes the most errors is not a typical *-ly* form.

Well is commonly confused with its adjective counterpart, *good*. As an adjective, *good* is used to describe nouns. In the following sentence, *good* describes the noun *pasta:* The pasta you made last night was *good*. In the following sentence, *good* describes the verb *played*, which is incorrect: I played *good* in the basketball game. The correct word to use in such instances is the adverb *well*. Written correctly, the sentence would read, "I played *well* in the basketball game."

PREPOSITIONS

Prepositions are connecting words that link a noun or pronoun to another word in a sentence. They are often used to show a relationship of space or time.

Examples

The <u>box</u> *on* your <u>desk</u> is your birthday present.
The <u>holiday</u> that follows immediately *after* your <u>birthday</u> is Valentine's Day.

The first sentence uses the preposition *on* to describe the spatial relationship between the *box* and the *desk*. The second sentence uses the preposition *after* to describe the time relationship between *holiday* and *birthday*. *On your desk* and *after your birthday* are prepositional phrases.

Common Prepositions

aboard	about	above	after	among	around	at	before
behind	below	beneath	beside	between	by	except	for
from	in	inside	into	like	of	off	on
outside	over	to	under	up	upon	until	with
within							

The two most common problems with prepositions are:

1. **Using them unnecessarily**

   Because it is so important in your essay to get to the point concisely, unnecessary prepositions should be avoided. Remember that when two or more prepositions are used together, chances are at least one is unnecessary.

   Poor form: I cleaned *up under* the kitchen cabinets.
   Good form: I cleaned *under* the kitchen cabinets.

   Poor form: She likes all sports *except for* soccer.
   Good form: She likes all sports *except* soccer.

   Poor form: They looked *outside of* the house for the lost cat.
   Good form: They looked *outside* the house for the lost cat.

2. **Confusing prepositional phrases**

   Certain words must always be followed by certain prepositions. These necessary prepositions are always used in combination with their respective supported words. Below are two examples of required prepositions—the preposition is in italics and the supported word is underlined. It is important to remember that they must always be used together:

   You must <u>account</u> *for* every item in your club's budget.
   The meal <u>consists</u> *of* eight separate courses.

   Common prepositional phrases:

account for	agree upon	angry with	argue about
compare to	correspond with	differ from	different than
identical to	independent of	interested in	speak with

Alternate Endings

Of all the rules governing prepositions, none is more famous than: *Never end a sentence with a preposition!* While this rule holds true for many situations, it is not an absolute. It is perfectly acceptable to end a sentence with a preposition, especially in your essay, if it makes the sentence flow better. For example, in popular speech, it sounds much more natural to say "That's all I can think of" than "That's all of which I can think."

The best technique for deciding to keep or remove prepositions at the end of sentences is to use your ear. What would the statement sound like if you kept—or dropped—the preposition? Does it sound like *you*, or does it sound like a college professor? Prepositions should not be used in an attempt to add importance or weight to your writing.

Many times short questions are ended in prepositions. Here are some acceptable and unacceptable examples. Note that the unacceptable sentences could be improved simply by dropping the preposition at the end.

Good Form
Does he have anything to worry *about?*
What did you use to make it *with?*
What is the report comprised *of?*

Poor Form
Is the extra-credit project over *with?*
Where is the stadium *at?*
Where do you want to go *to?*

► DANGLING PARTICIPLES AND MISPLACED MODIFIERS

Dangling participles and misplaced modifiers, though sometimes difficult to recognize, are easily fixed by rearranging word order. A **dangling participle** is a phrase or clause with a verb ending in *-ing* that does not refer to the subject of the sentence it modifies. Since it is so critical that your reader understand your point easily and exactly, dangling modifiers (and indeed any ambiguous language) must be avoided.

Incorrect: While working on his English assignment, Tony's computer crashed. (Was the computer working on the assignment?)
Correct: While Tony was working on his English assignment, his computer crashed.

Note that correcting a dangling participle involves adding and/or rearranging the words in a sentence to make the meaning clear.

Incorrect: While practicing outside with the soccer team, the noisy construction job distracted Jim.
Correct: While Jim was practicing outside with the soccer team, he was distracted by the noisy construction job.
OR
The noisy construction job distracted Jim while he was practicing outside with the soccer team.

A **misplaced modifier** is a word or phrase that describes something, but is in the wrong place in the sentence. It isn't dangling; no extra words are needed; the modifier is just in the wrong place. The danger of misplaced modifiers, as with dangling modifiers, is that they confuse meaning.

> **Incorrect:** I had to have the cafeteria unlocked meeting with student government this morning.

Did the cafeteria meet with student government? To say exactly what is meant, the modifying phrase "meeting with student government" should be moved to the beginning of the sentence.

> **Correct:** Meeting with student government this morning, I had to have the cafeteria unlocked.

NOUN AND VERB AGREEMENT

Nouns and verbs must agree in number, meaning a singular noun takes a singular verb, and a plural noun takes a plural verb. To achieve subject-verb agreement, first determine whether your subject is singular or plural, and then pair it with the correct verb form.

> **Incorrect:** Tim and Fran *is* a great couple.
> **Correct:** Tim and Fran *are* a great couple. (plural subject takes plural verb)

> **Incorrect:** One of my friends *are* going to your school.
> **Correct:** One of my friends *is* going to yourt school. (singular subject takes singular verb)

Agreement may be difficult to determine when the noun follows the verb. Common examples include sentences that begin with *there is* and *there are*, and *here is* and *here are*. When editing your work, remember to first determine whether your subject is singular or plural, and then match it to the correct verb.

> **Incorrect:** There *is* too many meetings scheduled on Tuesday morning.
> **Correct:** There *are* too many meetings scheduled on Tuesday morning.

> **Incorrect:** Here *are* the report you asked me to write.
> **Correct**: Here *is* the report you asked me to write.

> **NOUN AND VERB AGREEMENT CHECKLIST**
>
> The more complex the sentence, the more difficult it is to determine noun/verb agreement. Here are some guidelines that may help you:
>
> ✔ If a compound, singular subject is connected by *and*, the verb must be plural. (Both the 10-speed *and* the hybrid *are* appropriate for the bike race.)
>
> ✔ If a compound, singular subject is connected by *or* or *nor*, the verb must be singular. (Neither the 10-speed *nor* the hybrid *is* appropriate for a trail race, however.)
>
> ✔ If one plural and one singular subject are connected by *or* or *nor*, the verb agrees with the closest subject. (Neither a fast bike *nor perfect trails are* going to help you to win if you do not train.)

▶ ACTIVE VERSUS PASSIVE VOICE

The active voice is much more effective in conveying your personality through your essay. Not only is the active voice clearer and more direct, but it conveys your meaning more easily. In the active voice, you literally become the source, or cause, of the action.

In the passive voice, the subject (most often *you*) is acted upon. Sentences written in the passive voice tend to be too wordy, or lack focus. For these reasons, it should be used only when necessary. The good news is that passive-voice errors are easy to omit from your writing.

Compare these sentences:

Active: My friend asked for another helping.
Passive: Another helping was asked for by my friend.

Active: I misplaced my wallet.
Passive: My wallet was misplaced by me.

Active: The administration has selected three finalists for the open position.
Passive: Three finalists for the open position have been selected by the administration.

Note the simplicity and directness of the first sentence in each pair. The second sentences, written in the passive voice, are clunky and noticeably longer.

▶ SENTENCE STRUCTURE

A complete sentence requires a noun and verb, and expresses a fully developed thought. The two most common mistakes at the sentence level are extremes. Sentence fragments stop too quickly; they are phrases that are not whole thoughts. Run-on sentences don't stop soon enough; they include two complete clauses or sentences.

SENTENCE FRAGMENTS

A sentence fragment is a group of words that, although punctuated as a sentence, does not express a complete thought. Fragments are often missing a subject or verb, and may be dependent clauses. Fragments also can be phrases or parts of other sentences.

Examples

At the zoo.
Cried a lot.
Can't go to the store.
When we finished the game.

RUN-ON SENTENCES

A run-on sentence is made up of two or more independent clauses or complete sentences placed together into one sentence without proper punctuation.

Examples

We were hungry and John was tired so we had to stop at the first rest area that we saw.

Kim studied hard for the test that's why he got an A.

Patty took flying lessons every Saturday so she couldn't go to the picnic and she couldn't go to the graduation party either but she has already signed up for another group of flying lessons because she likes it so much.

Here are a few ways to correct run-on sentences.

1. Break up the run-on sentence into two or more complete sentences.
2. Use a comma and a conjunction (*and, or, nor, for, so, but, yet*) to set apart an independent clause.
3. Break up the sentence by inserting a semi colon between two clauses.
4. Use a dash to separate parts of the sentence.
5. Add a dependent clause (use words such as *because, after, since,* and *while*).

▶ VERB TENSE SHIFTS

Unnecessary shifts from one tense to another sound unskilled, and may obscure meaning. For instance, when describing an event in the past, all verbs should be in the past tense. This seems like an obvious point, but tense shifts account for a large share of grammatical errors.

Examples

Incorrect: When we finished our lunch, we *decide* to take a walk.
Correct: When we finished our lunch, we *decided* to take a walk.

Incorrect: Last year the governor said he *is campaigning* for our candidate.
Correct: Last year the governor said he *would campaign* for our candidate.
OR
Last year the governor said he *was campaigning* for our candidate.

▶ DOUBLE NEGATIVES

The use of double negatives is unnecessary and incorrect. As with verb tense shifts, the use of two negatives (such as "I won't never give up") in a sentence sounds incompetent, and obscures meaning. Eliminate them from your writing.

Incorrect: We hardly never see movies.
Correct: We hardly *ever* see movies.

Incorrect: There aren't no tickets left.
Correct: There aren't *any* tickets left.

Incorrect: Mary doesn't like neither of those books.
Correct: Mary doesn't like *either* of those books.

Incorrect: Vegans don't eat dairy products nor meat.
Correct: Vegans don't eat dairy products *or* meat.

TAKE NOTE

There are more negatives than just the obvious *no, not, never, neither*, and *nor.* Remember that *hardly* and *barely* are negatives, too. If you are using those words, you have a negative, so you do not need to double up.

▶ PUNCTUATION

There are dozens of different punctuation marks in the English language; those covered in this section are the ones that present the most challenges to their users. While the information may seem simple, and has been taught to you numerous times during your education, it pays to review it. With proper punctuation your writing will be more polished and technically correct, and will convey your voice more directly.

THE APOSTROPHE

Apostrophes (') are used to indicate ownership and to form contractions. Eight rules cover all of the situations in which they may appear.

1. Add *'s* to form the singular possessive, even when the noun ends in *s:*
   The *school's* lunchroom needs to be cleaned.
   The *drummer's* solo received a standing ovation.
   Mr. Perkins's persuasive essay was very convincing.

2. A few plurals not ending in *s* also form the possessive by adding *'s:*
   The *children's* toys were found in every room of the house.
   The line for the *women's* restroom was too long.
   Men's shirts come in a variety of neck sizes.

3. Possessive plural nouns already ending in *s* need only the apostrophe added:
   The *customers'* access codes are confidential.
   The *students'* grades improved each semester.
   The flight *attendants'* uniforms were blue and white.

4. Indefinite pronouns show ownership by the addition of *'s:*
   Everyone's hearts were in the right place.
   Somebody's dog was barking all night.
   It was *no one's* fault that we lost the game.

5. Possessive pronouns never have apostrophes, even though some may end in *s:*
   Our car is up for sale.
   Your garden is beautiful.
   His handwriting is difficult to read.

6. Use an *'s* to form the plurals of letters, figures, and numbers used as words, as well as certain expressions of time and money. The expressions of time and money do not indicate ownership in the usual sense:

She has a hard time pronouncing *s's*.
My street address contains three *5's*.
He packed a *week's* worth of clothing.
The project was the result of a *year's* worth of work.

7. Show possession in the last word when using names of organizations and businesses, in hyphenated words, and in joint ownership:
   Sam and Janet's graduation was three months ago.
   I went to visit my *great-grandfather's* alma mater.
   The Future Farmers of America's meeting was moved to Monday.

8. Apostrophes form contractions by taking the place of the missing letter or number. Do not use contractions in highly formal written presentations.

   Poor form: *We're* going out of town next week.
   Good form: *We are* going out of town next week.

   Poor form: *She's* going to write the next proposal.
   Good form: *She is* going to write the next proposal.

   Poor form: My supervisor was in the class of *'89*.
   Good form: My supervisor was in the class of 1989.

ITS VERSUS IT'S

Unlike most possessives, *its* does not contain an apostrophe. The word *it's* is instead a contraction of the words *it is*. The second *i* is removed, and replaced by an apostrophe.

When revising your writing, say the words *it is* when you come across *it's* or *its*. If they make sense, you should be using the contraction. If they don't, you need the possessive form, *its*, without an apostrophe.

THE COMMA

Correct usage of commas (,) is not as critical to the meaning of your sentences as it is with other punctuation marks. However, they can be used to convey your voice as they speed up or slow down the pace of your sentences. Consider the difference in tone of the following example:

Sentence A: During my junior year, I attended a conference in Washington, D.C., where student delegates from every state presented their ideas.

Sentence B: During my junior year I attended a conference in Washington, D.C. where student delegates from every state presented their ideas.

Sentence A sounds more deliberate, giving a little more information with each clause. Sentence B reads quicker, conveying the information faster and with equal weight on each part.

In addition to helping to convey your voice and personality, commas are often misused. There are two common errors that all college-bound students should be aware of: the comma splice, and the serial comma.

Comma Splice

A comma splice is the incorrect use of a comma to connect two complete sentences. It creates a *run-on sentence*. To correct a comma splice, you can either:

- replace the comma with a period, forming two sentences
- replace the comma with a semicolon
- join the two clauses with a conjunction such as *and, because,* or *so*

Comma splice: Our school received an award, we raised the most money for the local charity.
Corrected sentence: Our school received an award. We raised the most money for the local charity.
OR
Our school received an award; we raised the most money for the local charity.
OR
Our school received an award because we raised the most money for the local charity.

Serial Comma

A serial comma is the one used last in a list of items, after the word *and*. For instance, in the following example, the comma after *apples* is the serial comma:

At the store, I bought bananas, apples, and oranges.

The lack of a serial comma can cause confusion. In the sentence, *Cindy, Ann, and Sally were hired to work in the college counselor's office*, the message is straightforward. But if the serial comma is dropped, it could be understood as Cindy being told that Ann and Sally were hired.

Cindy, Ann and Sally were hired to work in the college counselor's office.

While its use has been debated for centuries, the serial comma clarifies the meaning of sentences. Therefore, you should use it consistently whenever writing a list.

THE COLON

Colons (:) appear at the end of a clause and can introduce:

- A list when the clause before the colon can stand as a complete sentence on its own
  Incorrect: The classes he signed up for include: geometry, physics, American literature, and religion.
  Correct: He signed up for four classes: geometry, physics, American literature, and religion.

- A restatement or elaboration of the previous clause
  Incorrect: Shari is a talented hairdresser: she is also the mother of two children.
  Correct: Shari is a talented hairdresser: she attends a seminar each month and has been a professional for over twenty years.

  Incorrect: My teacher wasn't in class today: he graduated Summa Cum Laude.
  Correct: My teacher wasn't in class today: he had to fly to Houston to present a paper.

Colons have the effect of sounding authoritative. They present information more confidently and forcefully than if the sentence were divided in two other types of punctuation marks. Consider the following:

My teacher wasn't in class today: he had to fly to Houston to present a paper.
My teacher wasn't in class today. He had to fly to Houston to present a paper.

The first example, with the colon, has the tone that conveys, "I know why this happened, and I am going to tell you." It sounds more authoritative. This can be effective in your essay, but because you never want to appear pompous, it should be used sparingly.

THE SEMICOLON

Semicolons (;) may be used in two ways: to separate independent clauses, and to separate the items in a list when those items contain commas.

- Use semicolons to separate independent clauses.

  Case: Use a semicolon to separate independent clauses joined without a conjunction.

  Example: Four people worked on the project; only one received credit for it.

  Case: Use a semicolon to separate independent clauses that contain commas, even if the clauses are joined by a conjunction.

  Example: The strays were malnourished, dirty, and ill; but Liz had a weakness for kittens, so she adopted them all.

  Case: Use a semicolon to separate independent clauses that are connected with a conjunctive adverb that expresses a relationship between clauses.

  Example: Victoria was absent frequently; therefore, she received a low grade.

- Use semicolons to separate items in a series that contain commas.

  Case: Use a semicolon to show which sets of items go together.

  Examples: The dates for our meetings are Monday, January 10; Tuesday, April 14; Monday, July 7; and Tuesday, October 11.

  She has lived in Omaha, Nebraska; Nutley, New Jersey; Amherst, Massachusetts; and Pensacola, Florida.

▶ CAPITALIZATION

Capitalization is necessary both for specific words and to start sentences and quotes. However, many writers overuse it, and thus appear overly casual. There are just six occasions that require capitalization:

1. the first word of a sentence
2. proper nouns (names of people, places, and things)
3. the first word of a complete quotation, but not a partial quotation
4. the first, last, and any other important words of a title
5. languages
6. the pronoun *I*, and any contractions made with it

▶ FOR YOUR REVIEW

- Pronouns, adjectives, adverbs, and prepositions are the most challenging parts of speech, accounting for a majority of usage errors. Learn the common errors to eliminate them from your writing.

- A dangling participle is a phrase or clause, using a verb ending in *-ing* that does not refer to the subject of the sentence it modifies. A misplaced modifier is a word or phrase that describes something, but is in the wrong place in the sentence. Both create ambiguity and can change the meaning of a sentence.

- Nouns and verbs must agree in number, meaning a singular noun takes a singular verb, and a plural noun takes a plural verb.

- The active voice is not only clearer and more direct, but it conveys your meaning more easily. Use it instead of the passive voice whenever possible.

- Avoid the two most common mistakes at the sentence level: sentence fragments and run-on sentences. Be certain each sentence contains one complete thought.

- Be consistent with verb tenses. Do not shift from one tense to another unless it is necessary.

- The use of double negatives is unnecessary and redundant. As with verb tense shifts, the use of two negatives (such as "I won't never give up") in a sentence sounds incompetent and can obscure meaning.

- Proper punctuation makes your essay more polished and technically correct, and it helps to convey your voice.

- There are six occasions that require capitalization. Using capitalization in any other way can make your writing appear too casual, or even sloppy.

Revising, Editing, and Proofreading

Many writers are tempted to skip the revising, editing, and proofreading steps, feeling intimidated by the thought of reworking their writing, and hoping their essays are "good enough." This chapter makes it easier to polish your essay by following simple guidelines. It includes many ideas that can quickly improve the quality of your writing, even if you feel your rough draft is close to perfect. There is no excuse for submitting an essay that is not the very best writing you are capable of.

Once you have a rough draft of your essay, you can begin to transform it into a polished piece of writing. The polishing process consists of three steps: revising, editing, and proofreading. Think of them as using different strengths of magnifying glasses to your essay. Revision looks at your essay through a lens that lets you see it as a whole; you will pay attention to the largest issues involved in its crafting. Have you addressed the topic? Is there a logical flow to your ideas or story? Is each paragraph necessary and properly placed?

Editing takes a closer look at your writing, through a stronger lens that highlights words and sentences. Are your word choices appropriate and fresh? Are there any repetitive or awkward sentences or phrases? Finally, the proofreading step puts your essay under the strongest lens. You will check *within* each word for errors in spelling and correct any other mechanics mistakes, such as grammar and punctuation.

Also included in this chapter are professional writers' and editors' tricks to help you with revising, editing, and proofreading. You will learn how the pros find and correct mistakes using the power of their word processors, and discover other ideas that help you locate errors that spell checks and grammar checks might miss.

▶ How to Revise

The revision process can seem overwhelming. From the Latin *revisere*, meaning to visit or look at again, revising involves a general examination of your writing. You need to look at your entire essay with fresh eyes and ears, checking to see if you have achieved your goal, and if any sections of the essay need improving.

When followed in order, these four revision strategies will help you clean up your essay and prepare it for editing and proofreading.

1. Put down your essay, and do not look at it for at least one day before revising. Masha Zager, a professional writer, says, "after I complete a first draft, I wait for two or three days before looking at it again. If I try to revise it too soon, I miss all kinds of errors. A couple of days away gives me a 'fresh eye' that's almost as good as having another person read my work."

2. Read it through once, imagining you are reading it for the first time. Editor Jen Ballinger even suggests reading it aloud. She notes, "it's amazing what you can catch that didn't 'sound' funny or awkward when you were reading it silently."

   High school senior Liz Abernathey waited a few weeks before rereading her rough draft. "When I took it out again, I saw some things that could be changed that I hadn't seen before. Putting the essay away for a while, and returning to it with fresh eyes, was very helpful. I recommend it to everyone who's writing an essay."

3. Note your reactions to the essay, and answer the following:
   - Does the content of your essay address or match the topic? (see Chapter 6)
   - Will your essay help you stand out? Is it memorable and interesting?
   - Would any reader(s) understand everything you have written, or are some points in need of clarification? (Chapter 2 deals with clarity)
   - Is the introduction a good "hook" that draws the reader into the essay, or could it be eliminated? (see Chapter 6)
   - Does the first paragraph include a clear thesis statement and touch on the major points of the essay?
   - Does your writing flow? Does it follow a logical progression, with each paragraph and point made in the right place?
   - Are the points you make supported by examples and details, and are all of the details necessary?
   - Does your writing strike the right balance between formality and informality?

- Does your conclusion make sense after the preceding paragraphs? Is it strong, or just a wrap-up of what you have already said? (Chapter 6)
4. Make any necessary modifications, and be willing to add and/or remove writing that isn't working. By revising on the computer, it is simple to make changes, see if they improve the essay, and then save the changes or try again. For example, if a point is not made clearly and directly, or if it is too general, insert a phrase or a sentence to clear it up.
   - Compare: I stay in shape for my sports teams all year.
   - With: I stay physically active during the year. I play football and basketball, and in the off-season run and lift weights.

The first sentence is vague, and tells very little about the author. By adding the types of teams, and the specific things the writer does to stay in shape, year-round, the reader better understands the point, and the writer.

In other instances, your point may get lost if you go off on a tangent, or include information that doesn't support it. In this case, you should delete the unnecessary words, phrases, or sentences. In the following example, a sentence about green tea simply clutters the paragraph. Compare the revised sentences to see how the author tightened up her essay.

> The day after that, I walked over to my neighbor's house and discussed with her the history of her property. She made us some green tea, which really hit the spot on such a chilly, fall day. During the course of our discussion I found out that in the early nineteen hundreds the land was part of the sprawling Mitchell dairy farm.

> The next day, I walked over to my neighbor's house and discussed with her the history of her property; it turned out that in the early nineteen hundreds the land was part of the sprawling Mitchell dairy farm.

▶ HOW TO EDIT

When you edit, you read through each paragraph of your essay a number of times, paying careful attention to your sentences and the words that comprise them. While some people can edit effectively on the computer, many others work better on a hard copy. Unlike revising, which entails the possible reworking of large parts of your essay, editing is a word-by-word and sentence-by-sentence task. Taking pencil to paper may help you focus more closely on the pieces that make up your essay, rather than the work as a whole.

As you read the hard copy of your essay, pencil in hand, circle any problems as you encounter them. You might also want to make a quick note in the margin with an idea or two about how to improve the problem(s). Ask yourself the following questions:

- Do I repeat myself? Rework your point so that you say it well the first time and remove any repetitious words and phrases.
- Do I have enough details? Look through your essay for generalities and make them more specific.
- Do I reinforce each point with a concrete and/or personal example?
- Is my sentence structure varied? Sentences should not be the same length, nor should they be repetitive in any other way, such as all beginning with "I."
- Are there any clichés or other types of overused language?
- Do I use the active voice whenever possible?
- Are there too many or too few adjectives and adverbs?
- Are verb tenses consistent?
- Is the antecedent for every pronoun clear?

After you have read through your essay a few times and highlighted any areas that need improving, focus on one problem at a time. For instance, if you find that you have used the passive voice too often, review the section on active versus passive voice in Chapter 4 (page 45). Then, rework your problem areas as the writer did on the following sentences. Note the freshness and originality of the second example as compared to the first:

A moving speech was made by our principal, and there was much grief and love expressed in the tears of Al's friends.

I listen to our principal make a moving speech, and then see Al's friends break down as they try to express their love and grief for him.

If you find too much unoriginal language, review the section on clichés found in Chapter 3. Replace any overused phrases and images with fresh words that are uniquely your own. For example, the following sentence is stale and boring. It even seems self-conscious of this fact as the phrase "behind the scenes" is in quotation marks:

My interest in an accounting career was inspired predominantly by my parents' business. Throughout my childhood I was exposed to the "behind the scenes" aspect of operating a small family business, and took great interest in the financial component of the operations.

Here, the writer reworked the sentences, making them more personal and original. They follow the advice of showing rather than simply telling, using sensory images to bring the reader into the scene (see Chapter 2 for a review of pinpointing, or replacing vague language with words and phrases that are more specific).

> Some of my earliest memories are of sitting behind the counter in my family's feed store. I would listen to the ring of the cash register, and watch as my mother carefully entered the sale in a large book. I became fascinated with the rows of numbers—a fascination that continues to this day as I plan a career in accounting.

The goal of editing is to make certain your essay works well on the sentence and word level. By checking and correcting your writing this closely, you will eliminate words and phrases that don't work, as well as unnecessary verb tense shifts, and confusing pronoun usage. Your writing will be fresh, original, and clear, and there will be enough variation to keep your audience interested.

STYLE GUIDES

Writers and editors use style guides to help maintain consistency, and to conform to formatting standards. These guides explain everything from how to write a bibliography to how to indent paragraphs and when to use commas. The three most popular and frequently used style guides are the MLA (Modern Language Association), Chicago Manual of Style, and APA (American Psychological Association). If you have not been directed to use one of these guides (or a similar one), you may consult one to answer any style questions that come up during the editing process.

In addition to using existing style guides, some writers and editors create their own style sheets that are specific to the project they are working on. These sheets are simply lists of key words and phrases that are repeated in the writing. For instance, if your essay is about former Pakistani Prime Minister Benazir Bhutto, you want to be sure you spell her name correctly each time it appears. Including it on a style guide gives you an easy reference.

You might also include the following on a style sheet:

◆ specific grammar points
◆ spellings
◆ abbreviations
◆ dates
◆ references
◆ weights and measures

▶ PROFESSIONAL REVISION AND EDITING TRICKS—HARNESSING THE POWER OF YOUR WORD PROCESSOR

Making large and small changes to your essay may seem frightening at first: what if you don't like what you have changed, and want to go back to your original form? Your word processor can make it easy when you understand how to use it to your advantage. The directions below show you how to employ some of the many features of your word processing program that can help you revise and edit.

When you have reread your essay and have an idea of the changes you want, or think you want to make, you can begin to add, delete, correct, and move text around. By using the "Track Changes" feature of your word processor, you can see what you have changed, and have the opportunity to save or undo your changes.

▶ TRACK CHANGES

Track Changes involves two different functions. One allows you to see what you are doing to the text as you revise and edit. The other lets you compare the "new" version to the original document. Therefore, the first step in using this feature is to copy your essay into a new document, creating a version that you can change and compare to the original (which is saved as a backup). To turn on the track changes feature, click on "tools," "track changes," then "highlight changes." Select "track changes while editing" and "highlight changes on screen" to see the feature at work while you revise and edit. You may also want to check "highlight changes in printed document" if you will work from a hard copy of your essay. "Highlight changes" must be checked if you wish to see the changes tracked as you make them.

The next step is to choose how you want track changes to work for you. Open the "working" version of your essay, then click on "Tools," "Options," and "Track Changes." You will see four categories for which you can choose options. The box below explains each function.

Inserted text	An underline is the default. You may change it to bold, italics, or double underline. Choose a specific color (rather than the default "by author") to mark all inserted text in that color.
Deleted text	The default is strikethrough (a line going through the word(s) you remove). If you select Hidden, the deleted text can be shown or hidden with the Show/Hide button on the Standard toolbar. To prevent the deleted text from appearing on the screen, select the ^ or # symbol.
Changed Formatting	"None" is the default. If you want to show any changes you make in formatting, select bold, italic, underline, or double-underline formatting.
Changed Lines	The default is outside border. Every paragraph that has a change shows a revision mark next to it. You can have these marks appear on the left, right, or outside borders.

Once you have revised and edited your essay, go back to the top of your document. Click on "tools," "track changes," and "accept or reject changes." Viewing options in this dialogue box are: "changes with highlighting," "changes without highlighting," or "original." You will be led to each change, with the option of accepting or rejecting it.

EDITING OPTIONS

Click on "tools," click on "options," click on "editing." There are eight editing options to choose from; four are pertinent to your essay.

Typing replaced selection	Turn this function on to highlight text to be removed, then type new text which will replace it.
Drag-and-drop text editing	This is perfect for moving words, phrases, and even paragraphs around in your essay. Highlight text to be moved, hold down left mouse button, move cursor to new location, and release the button to move the text.
Use smart cut and paste	Word automatically adjusts the spacing around deleted or inserted text when this function is on.
When selecting, automatically selects entire word	Click once anywhere on a word to select the whole word.

▶ How to Move or Change Text Using the Mouse

To edit existing text you must first select the text that you would like to change. While everyone familiar with basic word processing functions knows how to highlight using the mouse, there are a number of ways to select text that can save you time and prevent mistakes. To select:

- a single character: click and hold down the mouse button, then drag across the character.
- a single word: double-click on the word.
- one or more complete lines of text: move the cursor to the left side of the window until it turns into a right-pointing arrow. Click and hold the mouse button while dragging through the lines you want to select.
- a sentence: hold down the control key ("ctrl"), and click anywhere within the sentence.
- a paragraph: triple-click anywhere within it, or move the cursor to the left side of the window until it turns into a right-pointing arrow and double-click.
- multiple paragraphs: move the cursor to the left side of the window until it turns into a right-pointing arrow, double-click but hold down the mouse button on the second click. Drag up or down to select the desired paragraphs.
- a vertical block of text: hold down the control key ("ctrl") and drag across the desired text.
- the entire document: move the cursor to the left side of the window until it turns into a right-pointing arrow and triple-click, or choose "select all" from the "edit" menu.

Once you have selected text, there are a number of ways to manipulate it.

Change text
- Begin typing new text; old will be replaced.

Delete text
- Press the "delete" key.

OR
- Select "cut" from the "edit" menu.

Move text
- Use the "edit" menu to "cut" or "copy" the text. Next, click once at the desired location and select "paste" from the "edit" menu.

- Hold down the left mouse button while on the highlighted text, and move the cursor to the desired location. Then, release the button. This is known as "drag and drop."

Change case

- In the "format" menu, click on change case, select the desired change, and click on "ok."

HOW TO MOVE OR CHANGE TEXT USING KEYBOARD SHORTCUTS

Keyboard shortcuts are favored by professional editors, primarily because they are faster than using the mouse. They are simply combinations of keys that manipulate text. Shortcuts are listed in the word processing program's help files, and may be searched or printed. To find them:

- Press F1 (the shortcut key for Help).
- Click on the "Index" tab.
- In the field labeled "type the first few letters" type "Shortcut keys" or "Keyboard shortcuts."
- A list of topics will appear; double-click on the one that seems closest to the topic.
- You may also click on "viewing and printing shortcut keys" to get the entire list, and print it for easy reference.

A Few Helpful Shortcuts:

1. To highlight words, press "control" and "shift" simultaneously, and while holding them down, press an arrow key to move the highlighting to the left or right.
2. To change case, press shift + F3.
3. To find and replace, use ctrl + f and ctrl + h, respectively.
4. To delete a word, hit ctrl + del.
5. To move text, use F2.
6. To save changes, press ctrl + s.

▶ HOW TO PROOFREAD

Good proofreading involves far more than a simple run of spell and grammar check on your computer. In fact, those programs are not fool-proof, and therefore a reliance on them alone to find your errors is a mistake. However, they are not a bad place to start. Reread the advice for using spell check in Chapter 3 (page 36), and read the following guidelines for using computer grammar tools.

GRAMMAR CHECK TOOLS

You should always use a grammar check program on your writing. Grammar check can find possible errors, draw your attention to them, and suggest corrections.

The settings on these programs may be changed to check for only those elements that you specify; check for specific styles of writing, such as formal, standard, casual, and technical; and check for errors as you type, or when you are finished.

GRAMMAR CHECK SETTINGS

To modify the grammar check settings in Microsoft Word, open a blank document and:

1. Click on "Tools" on the toolbar at the top.
2. Select "Options."
3. Click on the "Spelling and Grammar" tab.
4. Click on "Settings" in the lower grammar section.
5. Read the list of options, and select those you want grammar check to look for
6. Click on "OK."

Although you should always use grammar check, you should not rely on it completely. Grammar programs make mistakes, both by missing errors, and by flagging "errors" that are actually correct. In fact, there have been a number of studies done comparing the effectiveness of various programs, and they perform about the same (fair to poor).

The first problem, missing errors, is illustrated by the following examples. A grammar check on the following sentence did pick up the subject/verb agreement error (*I is*), but did not notice the participle error (*I studying*).

I is ready to take the exam after I studying my notes and the textbook.

Similarly, the punctuation problems in the following sentence were not flagged.

The recipe, calls for fifteen ingredients and, takes too long to prepare.

When grammar check does highlight an error, be aware that it may, in fact, be correct. But if your knowledge of grammar is limited, you will not know whether to accept grammar check's corrections. To further complicate matters, you may be offered more than one possible correction, and will be asked to choose between them. Unless you are familiar enough with the specific problem, this may be no more than a guess. It is important to understand the type of error highlighted, and get more information if you are not sure about it. Consult the grammar advice in Chapter 4, as well as the resources listed at the end of the book.

BEYOND SPELL AND GRAMMAR CHECKS

When proofreading, use the professional tricks in the box below, and consider the following list. If you have any questions about possible grammar, punctuation, or spelling errors, *look them up*. Consult the resources at the end of this book for great ideas for online help and books that can answer your questions.

- Did you use any words incorrectly (check the lists of commonly confused and misused words on pages 22–26)?
- When using quotation marks, did you place all sentence-ending punctuation inside them?
- Did you use exclamation points only in dialogue?
- Is there a good balance of contractions (not too few or too many)?
- Do all subjects and verbs agree?
- Are there any double negatives? (see page 47)
- Are all apostrophes used correctly, especially when forming possessives?
- Do any lists of items contain mistakes in parallel structure?
- Have all hyphenated and compound words been used correctly?

PROFESSIONAL PROOFREADING TRICKS

1. **Take your time.** Studies show that waiting at least twenty minutes before proofreading your work can increase your likelihood of finding errors. Get up from your computer, take a break, or move on to some other task, and then come back to your writing.
2. **Read backward.** Go through your writing from the last word to the first, focusing on each individual word, rather than on the context.
3. **Ask for help.** A pair of fresh eyes may find mistakes that you have overlooked dozens of times; and one or more of your colleagues may be better at finding spelling and grammar errors than you are.
4. **Go under cover.** Print out a draft copy of your writing, and read it with a blank piece of paper over it, revealing just one sentence at a time. This technique will encourage a careful line-by-line edit.
5. **Watch the speed limit.** No matter which proofreading technique(s) you use, slow down. Reading at your normal speed will not give you enough time to spot errors.
6. **Know thyself.** Keep track of the kinds of errors you typically make. Common spelling errors can be caught by spell check if you add the word or words to the spell check dictionary. When you know what you are looking for, you are more likely to find it.

▶ FOR YOUR REVIEW

Finish your essay by revising, editing, and proofreading. Follow these guidelines:

- Put away your essay for at least 24 hours before beginning the revision process.
- Read through your entire essay as objectively as possible. Is it interesting? Does it relate to the topic or answer the question?
- Check to see if your essay flows. Does each point you make or idea you introduce follow the previous one well?
- Print out a hard copy of your essay for editing.
- Check for ideas and details: are there enough? Do they support your point?
- Make sure your writing is fresh. Eliminate repetition, clichés, and passive language.
- Use the powerful functions of your word processor to help you with revising and editing.
- Proofread your essay carefully for any errors in grammar, spelling, punctuation, and capitalization.
- Do not rely on computer spell check and grammar check programs to find all of your mistakes.
- Follow the professional proofreading tricks to eliminate all errors.

Untimed Essay Writing Strategies

ollege application essays and high school exit essays have much in common. They are both high stakes assignments that help determine your future course. It is important to write to the best of your ability, within the guidelines of the essay. Most of this chapter applies to both types of essays, even if some material seems geared only toward college admissions. Learning how to approach these essays, instead of jumping into writing as if it were a regular high school assignment, is vital to your score.

Thousands of secondary schools require a senior exit essay in order for a student to be eligible for graduation. Unfortunately, few of them follow the same format. They vary greatly in timing of the assignment, length, and choice of topic. Some schools assign an essay of a few hundred words, while others expect ten pages (approximately 2,000 words) or more. Topics could be personal and reflective, or strictly academic. It is vital that you gather all of the information you can about every requirement before beginning your essay. A great benefit of the exit essay is proximity to those who can help you. Take advantage of the fact that those who will score your essay are right in your school. If you have any questions, you can easily get answers.

College admissions essays are different. They are read and judged by strangers. If you have questions, it might be difficult to get an answer from the admissions committee. But enough schools have spoken out about what makes a great essay that it is relatively easy to understand what readers are looking for. The most important thing to remember is that, regardless of the topic, college admissions essays must be personal. The goal of the essay is not simply to show off your writing skills, but to tell the admissions committee something about you that will make them choose you. You are selling yourself. In order to do that best, you must begin by getting the applications you intend to submit either by mail or online. Read through the directions, noting submission deadlines, lengths, and topics. Begin thinking about what you could say about yourself that would convince an admissions officer that you are right for that school.

▶ LONG-TERM TIMING

Exit and college admissions essays should never be written at the last minute. It takes time to decide on a topic (if you are given a choice); choose an approach; organize your thoughts; write a rough draft; revise, edit, and proofread; and complete a final draft. The more time you spend on your essay, the greater your chances of success, especially if you do not consider yourself a strong writer.

Many schools begin the exit essay process in September. This is also the recommended month to start college admissions essays. Make an appointment on your calendar each week for work on your essay. You might spend the first few sessions exploring the topics, if you have a choice. Read the section in this chapter that explains what the topics require and how best to approach them. Then, move into prewriting, using one or more of the strategies explained in Chapter 1. Once you know what you want to write about, you can begin a rough draft.

By the beginning of November, college admissions essays should be ready for revising, editing, and proofreading. Exit essays are due at different times, but schedule at least a few weeks to work on your rough draft. Use Chapter 5 as a guide for these processes. When you finish proofreading, complete your final draft and prepare it for submission at least a few days before it is due. Long-term planning helps you finish on time, takes some of the stress out of the writing process, and improves your chances of getting a high score.

▶ PREWRITING STRATEGIES

Any of the six prewriting strategies explained in Chapter 1 can work well for exit essays and college admissions essays. But if your essay is personal, consider exploring your real subject first. Since that subject is you—your thoughts, experiences, likes and dislikes—it is wise to look inward with two great techniques: journaling and taking inventory.

JOURNALING

Keeping a journal might seem like an odd advice, unrelated to the major task you have to accomplish, but it is actually a great way to begin your essay, for two important reasons. First, your journal will sound like you, written in an authentic voice that should need very few adjustments when applied to the essay. Rachel Klein, a college counselor at Milton Academy in Milton, Massachusetts, advises her students to keep journals to help with essay writing because journals "give them back their own words." Journals, Klein says, are like "your mind coming out on paper." When you are writing your essay, you can use the journal as a reference for tone and word choices that convey your authentic voice.

The second reason for keeping a journal is that, as written with the journal prompts provided on page 70, it can be a great source of ideas. In your journal, you can write about what is important to you, your goals and aspirations, your values, and your take on everything from popular culture to current events. Coupled with the information you gather in your personal inventory, a journal is the perfect raw data from which to begin the essay writing process.

Journaling doesn't have to be elaborate, or time consuming. Take a minimum of five minutes a day to write or type something personal. To journal successfully, it must become a habit. In order to do that, you need to make the process as simple and painless as possible. Think about your habits, and which of the two journaling options best suits them. You can write in a book you have designated as your journal, or you can make journal entries on your computer, either in word processing documents, or in one of the many new online journal sites.

If you are writing, get a journal that is small enough to carry with you everywhere you go. When inspiration hits, you will be ready. Can't get started? Pick a time and place to write in your journal each day. If you are typing, set aside a specific time to journal. Open your journal document before going online to avoid distractions. Stick with it for the allotted time period.

If you are considering an online journal, visit www.blogger.com and/or www.livejournal.com to see how they are set up. Some sites require you to type entries while online, and others have downloadable diaries that may be added to at any time. A potential problem with these types of sites is the distractions. There are other diarist's entries to read, software to play around with, and features such as uploading pictures that can keep you from your real task. If you can't get right down to work, choose a handwritten or simple word processing journal.

Consider trying some of the following prompts to shake up an existing journal, or to get you started on a new one. If you are new to journaling, find some paper, or open a word processor document, and write about yourself, the world as you see it, a good thing that happened today, a bad thing that happened today. The subjects are limitless, but remember to keep it about *you*. Use the following prompts to help you if you are stuck, or want some direction for your writing.

- **Write a letter to someone who has had a significant influence on you.** Use as many details as possible to *show*, rather than *tell*, why they are so important to you.
- **Choose a current event and discuss its importance to you.** Be as personal as possible: how has the event changed your thinking? How does it make you feel? How has it impacted your daily life or your future plans?
- **Describe a risk you took, and what you gained or lost by taking it.** Did you learn something about yourself or the world? Are you a changed person because you took the risk? Was it worth it?
- **Choose a work of creativity (visual, musical, literary, scientific) that is of particular importance to you.** How has it influenced you? Describe it in great detail and remember to keep it personal.
- **Tell about a travel experience that affected you somehow.** Recount the experience as specifically as possible, using the five senses to detail it.
- **Describe a ritual you perform often that has meaning to you.** Think small. Do you meditate while setting the table? Listen to a certain kind of music while studying or reading? Cook something for yourself when you are stressed out? Don't worry if the ritual is quirky, or if it won't seem important to someone else.
- **Imagine a perfect world.** What does *perfect* mean to you? Get as detailed as possible. Aside from the requisite world peace and clean environment, think about the day-to-day things that would make a difference to you. Would every coffee maker have a "pause and serve" feature? Would your favorite band perform free concerts at your school every Saturday? Would everyone in your state, upon getting their driver's license, be given the car of their choice?

Once you begin the essay writing stage, your journal will become an invaluable tool. It can help you to use the right tone, neither too casual nor too formal, so that your essay sounds like you. While rereading it, make note of the words you use and what your voice sounds like when you write. Also, make note of the ideas and topics that hold your interest. Sometimes we are not aware of our feelings about something until we take the time to explore them. Use your journal entries to search for possible essay material.

PERSONAL INVENTORY

The personal inventory in this section is designed to help you mine your life for raw material that you can use in your essay. Although you won't use all, or even most, of the information you gather, be willing to explore many possibilities before narrowing down your essay topic.

KEEP IN MIND . . .

Although you should include as much information as possible in a college admissions essay, keep in mind a number of important qualities that readers are looking for. The qualities you will be rated in include:

creative, original thoughts	academic achievement
motivation	written expression of ideas
self confidence	disciplined work habits
independence, initiative	potential for growth
intellectual ability	

What activities and experiences can you write about that highlight one or more of these? How can you show (rather than tell) in your essay that you have these qualities? Keep them in mind when filling out your inventory.

To complete the personal inventory, you will need six sheets of paper, one for each of the following sections. List anything and everything that comes to mind for each section, leaving a few lines between each entry (so you can fill them out with details later).

1. *History*

   Think back to your earliest memory, and go from there. Move chronologically, cataloguing events in your life, until you reach the most recent one(s). Don't limit yourself to dramatic or life-altering experiences. Spend the most time on the past few years, unless you already know you will write about an event from your childhood.

2. *Achievements and Accomplishments*

   List all awards or other commendations you have received (academic, extra-curricular, etc.). Include goals you have reached or accomplished, that may not have been recognized by others. What has been important to you and your personal growth? What achievements are you most proud of?

3. *Activities*

   Outside the classroom, what have you spent your time doing? These may be one-time or on-going activities. Keep in mind, but don't limit yourself to: sports, civic groups, travel, volunteer work, art projects, technology, or religious groups. Why did you start the activity, and, if applicable, why do you continue with it? Remember, many of these are listed in other places on your application. Think about things you have done that are not mentioned elsewhere, or not given significant attention, on the rest of the application. Here is where you can expand.

4. *Influences*

   Make a list of the people, events, works of art, literature, and music that have affected you.

5. *Skills*

What are you good at? You may want to ask friends and family members to help with this. Skills may be those acquired through learning and practice, such as playing an instrument, or personal attributes, such as leadership, or willingness to follow the "road not taken."

6. *Passions*

What makes your blood boil or your heart beat faster? Is there a sports team you follow with fervor, a book you have read ten times, a topic of local, national, or global importance that gets you riled up? You may have listed these in other sections above; repeat them here because this category examines them from a different point of view.

▶ UNDERSTANDING THE TOPICS

This section explains seven topics frequently used on college application essays. They include a free choice topic, which is often used for exit essays. The first five come from the Common Application, which is currently accepted by over two hundred colleges and universities. Schools that have their own applications often use these same topics as well.

1. *Evaluate a significant experience, achievement, risk you have taken, or ethical dilemma you have faced, and its impact on you.*

The last phrase is critical: whatever you choose to write about (the "cause"), you must show its impact upon you (the "effect"). Your experience need not be earth-shattering; remember that small and seemingly insignificant can be better. You are guaranteed to write an original essay if you focus on something that you alone experienced or find significance in.

Writing an essay on what it felt like to drive a car alone for the first time, for instance, or why you enjoy preparing a favorite recipe, can show your creativity and your willingness to see the big picture. Perhaps the cooking experience showed you how a bunch of little steps add up to something big, or how a series of words on paper can connect you with your ethnic heritage. In other words, readers don't want to know about how you took first prize in the Mozart Piano Competition. If you want to write about piano playing, you could briefly mention the prize, but be sure to explain how the rigors of practice, the wisdom of your teacher, and the knowledge of musical composition have changed you for the better.

2. *Discuss some issue of personal, local, national, or international concern and its importance to you.*

Many experts caution against writing on this topic unless the issue has had a profound and highly personal effect on you. It lends itself to clichés ("why I want world peace") and can steer you away from your task, which is to reveal something about yourself.

Another potential problem with this topic is that you can alienate yourself from your reader. You don't know if your essay will be read by a 20-something, a 70-something, democrat or republican, male or female. Be careful not to dismiss or harshly critique the other side of your argument while presenting your own.

Since this topic is not among the most popular, you may stand out simply by choosing it. Just avoid the potential problems, and display your knowledge of the issue, while keeping the focus highly personal.

3. *Indicate a person who has had a significant influence on you, and describe that influence.*

Be wary of choosing a famous person as an influence. The admissions officers have read many essays about Martin Luther King, Jr., Mother Theresa, and Charles Lindbergh. If you write about a famous person, you need to get highly creative in your explanation of *how* he or she influenced you.

Successful essays on this topic typically center on someone known personally to the writer (although be aware that parents are favorites with many essay writers, meaning again that you will need to be highly creative in order to write a unique essay). No matter whom you write about, remember that the question is a catalyst for revealing information about you, not about your role model. Do not simply describe the person. Show evidence of yourself throughout your essay by relating everything back to you.

4. *Describe a character in fiction, a historical figure, or a creative work (as in art, music, science, etc.) that has had an influence on you.*

As with number three above, you need to keep the focus on you, not the character or creative work. Your choice of topic does reveal something about you, but you need to reveal even more by showing how she/he/it has influenced you. This is not one of the most popular topics, so you will have a good chance of standing out just by choosing it. Just be certain to keep it personal.

5. *Topic of your choice.*

This question is found on dozens of applications (other than the Common Application) in many different forms. Massachusetts Institute of Technology (MIT) asks "We want to get to know you as a person. Make up a question that is personally relevant to you, state it clearly, and answer it. Feel free to use your imagination, recognizing that those who read it will not mind being entertained." Seton Hall University puts it this way: "The application lists several topic suggestions, but feel free to write about any subject that you feel is relevant and will enable us to get to know you."

As with the request for a writing sample below, this topic lends itself to essay "recycling." If you already have a well-written, vivid piece on something of great significance to you, something you know well, and that has changed or greatly impacted upon you, you may use it here.

6. *Why are you applying to our school?*

What they want to hear: that you will attend if they accept you, that you will graduate from their school, and that you have something meaningful to contribute to the school community.

This question requires research using resources other than the website and brochures or other published material generated by the school. Are there alumni or current students in your area? Talk to them about what the school is really like, and use this material when highlighting your particular strengths. Does the school host an international science fair every year? Mention it if you are dying to meet and speak with a renowned scientist who frequently attends. Does the literary magazine win top honors at the national level? Include some of your poetry and write about your dream of getting published and working in the publishing industry.

7. *Submit a writing sample.*

There are three ways to approach this, two of which can save you time by recycling essays you have already written. The first is to write a new essay specifically for the application, but that option doesn't make much sense when you probably have appropriate samples already written.

You may also submit the original copy of an essay you wrote for a class, with teacher comments. Be certain to use an essay that is on an interesting topic, and that got an A. The advantages to this choice are that it is fast and effectively gives you another teacher recommendation if the comments are positive, and he or she didn't already write one of your recommendations.

You may also submit a rewrite of an essay written for a class, improving it by incorporating teacher comments (which, in effect, gives you the use of an editor). There is no need to mention the grade the essay received, or the class or teacher it was required by.

Essays written for other college applications are also acceptable, as long as they are not geared specifically for another school.

▶ CONSIDERING THE TOPICS

When you examine each topic, it will become clear which one(s) allow you to present yourself and your story best. What topic can you make the best emotional connection with? That is the one that will connect with your readers, too. College counselor Dr. Beverly Lenny advises her students to "choose the right vehicle to express yourself. What you want to say is more important than the question itself."

Go back over the topics in the preceding section, adding any other topics your applications, or your school, may provide you with. Then:

1. For each different topic or question, use a separate sheet of paper, and write the topic at the top.
2. Write anything that comes to mind in response to that topic. Your ideas may be in the form of a neat list, moving from the most to least important, or they can be random, needing more organization later.
3. Get out your personal inventory and match information with the topics. Does your summer job at the local independent bookstore, and all you have learned from your eccentric boss, fit well with topic #3? What about your obsession with fashion photography? It could be narrowed down to a specific creative work or body of work (topic #4), or work well as a significant experience (topic #1) if you write about your visit to New York to attend a seminar at the Fashion Institute of Technology.

Once you have prewriting notes on each topic, answer the following:

- Can I answer the question or address the topic completely?
- Does the topic let me highlight something about myself that was not evident on the rest of the application?
- Is the topic about something personally significant and important to my life?
- Can I make the essay unique, easily avoiding clichés?
- Will my essay on this topic say something positive about me?
- Can I write about myself and this topic without bragging or overstating my importance?
- Will my essay on this topic hold the interest of the reader?
- Does the topic avoid potentially offensive subjects?

TOPICS THAT WORK

- ◆ Academic interests (if you are passionate about them), such as why you love calculus, the works of Stephen Crane, studying about the Civil War, etc.
- ◆ Anything personal that steers away from a "common mistake" (see box on page 77). Write about an emotional reaction to an event, a work of art, or another person.
- ◆ Success out of failure: what problem did you face that helped you learn a great lesson, and grow as a person? How did you turn an obstacle into an attribute or achievement? (But keep it positive; you don't want your essay to sound like a sob story or an excuse.)
- ◆ Small is fine. Most students in their late teens have not experienced a traumatic, life-changing event. Write about something you know, of great significance to you, while seemingly mundane or routine to everyone else.
- ◆ Something that gets you excited, something you are passionate about.

▶ MAKING THE CHOICE

For most students, it is becoming clear at this point which topic best suits their life, strengths, and experiences, lending itself to the most unique and insightful essay. However, if more than one topic seems like a good fit, go back to your inventory. Using a different colored highlighter for each topic, mark the information that could be used to write on that topic. To which topic can you bring the most actual experiences and concrete details?

Still not sure? Consider outlining and writing rough drafts of two essays. High school senior Liz Abernathey says she wrote four essays on different topics before coming up with one she liked. "After I wrote the first one, I reread it, and realized that I had told a memory of something I really liked, but nothing more. Rather than trying to fix it, I simply began again. I wrote another essay a few days later, and a similar thing occurred. After reading it, I just didn't feel a 'click.' This process happened until my fourth essay. Although I only had a rough draft, I knew I had hit upon something good. I felt the click. It just worked better than the other topics."

In the examples below, a student took the same information and applied it to two topics. Note that the second example, while still just notes, seems to lend itself to more actual experiences and concrete details.

Indicate a person who has had a significant influence on you, and describe that influence.

When my science teacher assigned a research paper on a scientist of our choice, I wasn't thrilled. I had no one in mind for the month-long project. I sat at the keyboard in the school library, looking for inspiration. Finally, I started a search for "women scientists." I found a hit with a quote from Al Gore, calling the mystery person "an outstanding role model for women scientists across America."

Who was she? The late Dr. Nancy Foster, former Assistant Administrator for Oceanic Services and Coastal Zone Management at the National Oceanic and Atmospheric Administration, and Director of the National Ocean Service. The more I read about this brilliant, dynamic woman, the more I became inspired. Not only did I feel impressed with and proud of her many accomplishments, but her story made me think that I could take my love of the ocean and its creatures and make it into a career as a marine biologist.

Evaluate a significant experience, achievement, risk you have taken, or ethical dilemma you have faced, and its impact on you.

When my science teacher suggested a class trip to Belize to study the marine ecosystem, I was excited. The thought of escaping the cold New England winter *for sun and sand was my first thought. Then, I wondered if I would be able to go SCUBA diving there, in a real ocean, after only four months of taking classes in the chilly pool at the local community center. Mr. Carlson told us that we would be making trips to the coral reef in Ambergris Caye, and writing up our findings as a report once we got back to school. I didn't know yet that the trip would begin to give direction to my life.*

AVOID THE MOST COMMON ESSAY BLUNDERS

Admissions Directors note that the worst essays usually:

- ◆ are depressing.
- ◆ paint an unflattering picture of the applicant.
- ◆ are completely impersonal or unoriginal.

While just about any experience can be the basis of a great essay, keep in mind the following tips:

- ◆ *Positive is probably better.* You could write a superb essay on the anxiety you have experienced as a teen (think cliché), or your struggle with depression, but think about your audience. How many times does an admissions officer want to read depressing topics?
- ◆ *Focus on the recent past.* Readers want to know about who you are today, not about your early childhood. Unless it has significant relevance to who you are today, skip it.
- ◆ *Keep unflattering experiences to yourself.* You want the readers to like you. Don't tell them about major screw ups or stupid things you did. You want to sound competent and responsible. See "success out of failure" above.
- ◆ *Avoid clichés!* "Peace in the Middle East," "Why my volunteer position helps me more than those I'm supposed to be helping," "How my friend's death taught me to enjoy life more," have all been done before, many times. Unless your take on a popular topic is highly original and highly personal, you run the risk of boring your audience. Showcase your uniqueness by steering clear of obvious topics and content.
- ◆ *Think local, not global.* Large societal or political issues are usually not personal. Subjects such as world peace, September 11, and Columbine have been expounded upon by experts every day in the media, and you probably do not have a unique perspective (unless you were personally involved, or directly impacted). Think specific and personal, rather than abstract and global.

◆ *Resist any temptation to brag.* Do not go overboard highlighting your achievements, and especially don't take credit for something you shouldn't. For example, did your team really win the state championship because of your leadership skills? There is a great difference between advocating for yourself and sounding pompous.

▶ PARTS OF THE ESSAY

There are three distinct parts to your essay: the introduction, body, and conclusion. In this section, winning strategies for each section are examined.

INTRODUCTION

Exit essays differ from admissions essays in that they are scored by a teacher or administrator from your school. This reader (or readers) will take time with your writing. In contrast, anonymous admissions officers typically spend just two or three minutes reading each application essay. While you can afford to write a standard introduction to an exit essay (one that spells out your argument), that technique doesn't work well for college admissions essays. Because of your readers' time constraints, your introduction must immediately entice him or her to read further. There are a number of effective methods for "hooking" your reader from the very first sentences of your essay.

The best way to write a compelling introduction is to *wait to write it until you have completed the rough draft of the rest of your essay*. Then, extract something from your writing to use as an opener. Here are some great ways to create a hook for your reader:

- **Get emotional.** Your reader will relate to your subject if you engage their emotions and cause them to make a connection with you and your writing. Think about beginning with the way you felt about something, rather than first describing or otherwise revealing that something.
- **Be mysterious or intriguing.** Your introduction needs to relate to the rest of your essay, but there can be a small detail that makes the admissions officers wonder what you are up to. Are you writing about how your music teacher has influenced you? You might begin by describing him playing his cello in a few detailed sentences. Don't mention that he is your teacher, or that he has helped shaped your love of music yet. The reader will wonder who the mystery man is, and want to read on to find out.
- **Give an anecdote.** A very short slice of life story that doesn't clue the reader in to where you are headed can be a great hook. Write about the last seconds of a basketball game, checking out your last customer of the day, your brilliant but disorganized teacher's lecture on Emerson. Admissions officers will have to keep reading to discover what you are writing about.

- **Ask a question.** "When have you ever heard of a basketball coach reading poetry to her team?" "Why would I want to give up my poolside summer as a lifeguard to work in a rundown school without air conditioning?" Take your subject, and first ask yourself what is unusual or in need of an explanation. Turn it into a question that does *not* have an obvious answer.

- **Cite an unusual fact.** Telling your reader something he or she doesn't know, and wouldn't guess, can compel her to read on. If you are writing about a travel experience, hunt down some statistics that might seem startling. "The U.S. Department of Transportation reported that during the month I was traveling, over 255,000 pieces of luggage were lost." Did your youth group volunteer with migrant farm workers picking oranges? A few minutes of research can help you begin your essay, "Florida's Valencia orange forecast for April was 86 million boxes."

BODY

The body of your essay should be the easiest part to write. Using your outline and notes, put down your thoughts in clear sentences that flow logically from one to another. Tell your story seamlessly, using transitions (see the list of transition words in Chapter 7, pages 90–91) to move from one point to the next. Remember that you are writing a rough draft; don't worry over every word. If you find weaknesses with your outline as you write, such as missing details or a paragraph that would work better in another part of your essay, make adjustments. Keep in mind though, there is plenty of time to refine your essay during the revision and editing processes.

Provide an obvious connection between your introduction and the body of your essay. Don't waste a dynamic start by dumping the reader into a new context that leaves her asking, "where am I?" Show clearly why you began as you did. For example, if you opened with a statistic (such as the introduction example about Valencia oranges), the next sentence must connect the numbers with your own experience. It might be, "My youth group had a hard enough time packing a dozen boxes of oranges a day. It's hard to imagine how many hours of work is represented by 86 million boxes."

Use concrete examples, details, and evidence to support the points you make in your essay. Review the section in Chapter 2 entitled "Modifiers Add Precision" for ideas that will help your writing come alive and be uniquely yours. That doesn't mean, however, that you should run to your thesaurus. Admissions directors and college counselors give this piece of advice often: do not use words specifically to show off your vocabulary, or to try to wow your reader. There is an important difference between using just the right word to convey meaning, and using a bigger, longer word when a simpler one will do.

Not convinced to put down your thesaurus? Here are three reasons to stop looking for and using so-called "big words."

1. **They sound pretentious.** Remember, you are supposed to sound like you, not a politician or chairman-of-the-board.
2. **They can sound ridiculous.** By using words that are not in your normal vocabulary, you run the risk of using them incorrectly.
3. **They may appear as a tactic.** Your reader might think you are trying to add weight with words because you are worried your essay isn't well written, or that your ideas aren't worth reading.

Look at the following examples:

To the point: I decided to keep it simple by packing only those things that I could carry in one suitcase.
Thesaurized: I determined to eschew obfuscation by packing only those things that I could transport in one valise.

To the point: In high school, I took my first accounting class and began to help my mother with the accounting tasks of the business.
Thesaurized: In secondary school I took my first accounting class and commenced to aid my mother with the accounting functions of the business.

To the point: At my summer job, I had the chance to learn about Information Technology as it relates to engineering.
Thesaurized: At my place of summer employment, I had the fortuity to obtain IT-related information as it pertains to the engineering field.

A WORD ABOUT PLAGIARISM

You are probably aware of the many Internet sites offering essays for sale, and sites and books claiming they have "essays that work." What you may not realize is that teachers, administrators, and admissions committees know about them, too. In fact, they can check suspicious essays against those found on the Internet and published in books. Having even a phrase or two in common with one of these essays constitutes plagiarism.

The advice is simple: write your own essay. Don't even waste your time reading other people's essays looking for ideas. It is one thing to read to understand the process, and another to read for ideas and words to take as your own.

The sample topics and excerpts in this chapter are included to show you how the pieces of these essays (used as examples throughout the book) work when they are part of a whole. They are not intended as source material for your essay. Remember that plagiarism is a serious academic offense, and will disqualify you from consideration by the school(s) to which you are applying. It is too high a price to pay after all of the work you have done to get yourself this far. Be certain your ideas and words are your own.

CONCLUSION

Your conclusion is the final impression left with your reader. End your essay memorably by avoiding these three conclusion blunders. You should avoid:

- **Answering the big questions.** If you wrote about a topic such as world peace or a personal tragedy, resist the temptation to give reasons or solutions. You don't need to explain why there is evil in the world, or how world hunger can be stopped.
- **Using clichés.** Too many essays end with "therefore," "in conclusion," or "in summary." End in your own voice, using fresh words and phrases.
- **Summarizing your essay.** The biggest blunder is when the essay is short enough that you can expect your reader to remember what you wrote a few paragraphs ago. Summaries are boring, and waste your opportunity to leave your reader with something memorable.

You want your conclusion instead to echo the dynamic start of your essay. How can you achieve that?

- **Continue your discussion.** Propose where it might lead, what it might mean to future generations, or how it might be resolved.
- **Make sense of what happened.** If you told a story that would benefit from an explanation of what it means to you in larger terms, take a few sentences to explain. What did you learn? How will you benefit from the experience?
- **Connect your content with the desire for a college education.** What does it say about your decision to apply, specifically, to their college?
- **Echo your introduction to provide balance.** Use some of the same words, phrases, or ideas mentioned in your first paragraph.
- **Bring the reader to the present day.** This works especially well if you wrote about something that happened in your past. What does it say about who you are now? How has it influenced the plans you are making for the future?
- **If it works well with your content, end with words on the subject said by someone famous.** Be certain the quote substantiates what you have said, and speaks obviously to your topic.
- **Enlarge your discussion by linking it to a wider context.** Your weeklong hands-on experience with the problems of a small group of migrant farm workers could conclude with a paragraph on the widespread nature of the problem.

DON'T REPEAT YOURSELF

The essay is not the place to repeat information that can be found elsewhere in your application. For instance, you have already listed your extra curricular activities and GPA, and they have been noted by the admissions committee. There is no need to remind them of these accomplishments. Use your essay to tell your readers something they don't already know about you. You only have a few hundred words to make your mark. Don't waste them on sentences such as: *As I pointed out in my list of extra-curricular activities, I was elected to student council four years in a row, and spent two years as president.*

▶ WRITING TO YOUR AUDIENCE

Exit essays are typically written for people you know, such as the English teachers in your high school. You might even know one or more of them quite well. But don't let that fact influence the tone of your essay. It is a serious assignment with high stakes attached. Now is not the time to be silly or otherwise informal. Aim for a balance between formality and informality, and keep in mind the following advice given for applications essays.

It's not easy to describe typical admissions directors. Most schools hire a mix of young and old, scholastic and athletic, alumni and not, conservative and liberal. What they have in common is an ability to spot good writing, and a willingness to make a connection with their applicants. Your job is to try to appeal to one or more of them.

College admissions committees are usually made up of between ten and twenty people. There is a Dean, or Director of Admissions, who leads a team of Assistant or Associate Directors. Some schools even hire senior interns, who are still working toward their degrees, to evaluate applications.

The committees vary a great deal in their makeup. Most schools now attempt to provide a diverse group, employing women and minorities. Each admissions director is typically in charge of a geographical area of the country, or of the world if the school draws or wants to draw international students. They travel to those areas to attend college fairs, conduct interviews, and speak at secondary schools. They are available to applicants to answer questions and give a better idea of what the school is like (especially if they are an alumni/ae).

When applications are submitted, the work of the committee goes into high gear. Some schools receive thousands of applications for a few hundred spots. Others are less selective, but still must evaluate each application they receive. Everyone on the committee gets hundreds of essays to evaluate, meaning they spend an average of two to three minutes reading each one.

Admissions directors do not read with a highly judgmental eye, ready to circle every dangling participle or toss your essay if they find an unclear pronoun reference. Instead, they read to find essays that they connect with. The connection is a feeling he or she gets from your writing. Your goal is to give them the sense, through your writing skills, that you are capable of a college workload, and have much to offer their school.

But remember that the essay is also referred to as a *personal statement*. The most important connection you can make is not between your reader and the intellectual argument you present, but rather an emotional or personal connection with the content of your essay. Simply put, a winning essay makes admissions directors like you.

SHOULD YOU USE HUMOR?

This is a tough question, and the simple answer is, probably not. A light-hearted, witty tone is fine if it fits with your subject. But resist the urge to tell a wild and crazy story, or to tell a straight story with jokes and puns thrown in. You don't know your reader's sense of humor. If he or she doesn't find it funny, you run the risk of looking foolish. Unless you are known for your great sense of humor, keep your tone upbeat, but leave out the jokes.

APPROPRIATE LEVEL OF FORMALITY

Your essay should strike a balance between formality and informality. You don't want to sound distant and stiff, like a college professor, but a slangy, highly informal tone is also inappropriate. Your voice should be another piece of personal information you share with the admissions committee. Let your reader hear you, not your impressive vocabulary or your attempt to sound like what you think they want to hear.

The balance you need to strike between formality and informality is simply the avoidance of one extreme or another. You are not writing to your best friend, nor are you writing an academic essay. Review some of your journal entries. These are written in the voice you want to use, with just the right level of formality.

CHECKLIST—FINDING THE APPROPRIATE LEVEL OF FORMALITY

Follow these guidelines to insure your tone is correct:

- Avoid slang words and phrases unless you are deliberately trying to imitate speech.
- A few contractions (*I'm, don't, who'd, shouldn't*) can help your essay from sounding too stiff.
- Aim to sound like a 17 or 18 year old (i.e., yourself).
- Don't use five words when one will get the point across, or use words considered archaic or pretentious (*according to*, not *as per*; *determine*, not *ascertain*; *think about*, not *cogitate*).

- If you are worried your writing is too stiff, rewrite a few paragraphs as a mock journal entry, then compare them to your essay. What words or phrases need toning down?

▶ FOR YOUR REVIEW

- Long-term planning will take some of the stress out of essay writing, and help you create the best essay you are capable of, error-free, and on deadline.
- Use the prewriting strategies of journaling and inventory-taking to gather possible subject matter for your essay.
- Study the different topics, and understand what each is asking you to write. If you are writing a college application essay, you must keep it personal no matter the topic.
- Choose a topic after you have tested a few. Your topic should be the one that lets you best tell your story.
- Write a compelling introduction that entices the reader to continue. Standard introductions (those that spell out what your essay will contain) are not only boring, but they could cause a reader to put down your essay.
- The body of your essay should follow seamlessly from one point to the next, and use details and examples for reinforcement.
- Don't use the thesaurus to add big words intended to impress.
- End with a dynamic, rather than a clichéd, conclusion. Leave a lasting impression on your reader by avoiding the obvious summary.
- Keep your audience in mind, and don't include anything that might offend or confuse.
- Use humor with caution.
- Tone and word choice should strike a balance between formality and informality.

Timed Essay
Writing Strategies

Writing an essay in an exam situation, with the clock ticking, is very different from other types of essay writing. Of course, the fundamentals of good writing do not change (which is why Chapters 1–4 apply to any type of essay). What changes is your approach. When you have just 25 minutes (SAT), 45 minutes (GED), or an hour (many state tests, such as Regents'), you must use your time wisely. Every minute counts.

The way to take full advantage of every minute is to prepare; gather all available information about the test beforehand, and develop a strategy that will take you through the essay writing process. Understand the topics, know how to organize your thoughts, and be able to expand prewriting notes into paragraphs. Take timed practice exams to get used to the situation, and also to identify your strengths and weaknesses. The weeks before the exam are when you should figure out which topics you write best on, and which grammatical errors you make most frequently. When you take a timed essay exam, preparation can mean the difference between a great score and a poor one.

▶ TYPES OF EXAMS

While most of the information in this chapter applies to every type of timed essay writing situation, there are specifics for each test that you should be aware of. In this section you will learn the general features of the most common timed essays, as well as how to get the most up-to-date information about topics and any changes made to the tests.

GED

The General Educational Development (GED) test contains a 45 minute-writing section in which test takers must develop an expository essay which includes personal observations, knowledge, and experiences. The typical GED essay is about 250 words in length, written on one of five given topics. The official GED Testing Service website offers links to your jurisdiction's testing program, which may differ slightly from that of other states. Check www.acenet.edu/clll/ged/index.cfm for the latest information.

Those who score the GED essay read between 25 and 40 essays an hour. They look for:

- well-focused main points
- clear organization
- development of ideas
- appropriate sentence structure and word choice
- correct punctuation, grammar, and spelling

SAT I

With just twenty-five minutes to write, you will not be expected to turn in a final draft essay when taking the SAT I. Minor errors in grammar, usage, and mechanics are not weighed against you. Scorers instead read the essay to get an overall impression of your writing ability. They look for evidence of critical thinking: how well did you respond to the topic, develop a point of view, and use appropriate examples and evidence to support your position? Is your essay clearly focused, and does it transition smoothly from one point to the next? Do you show evidence of having a varied and intelligent vocabulary?

Since readers will look at dozens of essay, an hour, it is important to make your essay stand out. This is best done through the use of examples and evidence. Don't just strive to be technically perfect, or try to discuss important topics such as world history or scientific advances (unless you are passionate about them). Stand out by using specifics that make the essay uniquely yours.

The latest information on the SAT I essay may be found at www.collegeboard.com.

REGENTS' AND OTHER EXIT EXAMS

More than twenty-five states, including California, Alaska, North Carolina, and Texas, require a passing grade on an exit exam to be eligible for high school graduation. These tests vary, so it is important to get specific information about the test you are preparing to take. However, most exit exams allow 60 minutes to develop an essay based on one of a choice of topics. A list of topics for Georgia's Regents' exam, for example, may be found at: www.gsu.edu/~wwwrtp/topics.htm (but remember to check with your school regarding the test you will be given).

A typical exit essay is approximately 1,500 words, and is either expository or persuasive. Other possible topics include responses to literature, biographical narratives, and even business letters. Those who grade exit essay exams ask:

- How well did you address the topic?
- Were your ideas organized?
- Did you develop major points and support them with details and examples?
- Were your word choices and sentence structure effective and varied?
- How consistent was your style (paragraphing), grammar, spelling, and punctuation?
- Did you express yourself freshly and uniquely?

▶ TYPES OF ESSAYS

You have been assigned dozens of essays during high school. They might have been a response to something you read, an argument about a particular topic, or an explanation of an event or other subject of study. In fact, there are countless types of essays. However, almost all timed essay exams fall into one of two major categories: expository or persuasive. In fact, the SAT I essay exclusively calls for persuasive essays.

EXPOSITORY

An expository essay gives directions, instructions, or explanations. It informs by presenting the writer's knowledge about the topic to the reader. You might be asked to *define, compare* and/or *contrast*, or *explain* cause and effect. In fact, think of the verbs used in your topic as *key words* that clue you in to the fact that you are being asked to write an expository essay. These key words include:

- **compare:** examine qualities or characteristics to note and discuss similarities and differences
- **contrast:** examine two or more ideas, people, or things, stressing their differences

- **define:** give a clear, authoritative meaning that identifies distinguishing characteristics
- **describe:** relate the details that make the subject in question unique
- **diagram:** create a graphic organizer (see Chapter 1, page 7) that explains your answer
- **discuss:** examine the subject(s) thoroughly, and give a detailed explanation of its strengths and weaknesses
- **enumerate:** determine the points you must make, and present them in a list or outline form
- **explain:** clarify meaning in a straightforward fashion, paying attention to the reasons for a situation (review Chapter 2, page 13, about Qualifying and Quantifying)
- **illustrate:** use examples, graphic organizers, evidence, or analogies to give meaning or answer a problem
- **interpret:** explain the meaning of something or solve a problem using personal opinions, judgments, or reactions
- **list:** see *enumerate*
- **narrate:** explain an occurrence by describing it as a series of chronological events
- **outline:** describe in an organized fashion, systematically, highlighting only the major points (details not necessary)
- **relate:** explain the associations or connections between two or more things, events, circumstances, or even people; may also be used to mean *narrate* (see above)
- **recount:** see *narrate*
- **review:** critically examine the topic, event, idea, or thing in question, discussing major points and their strengths and/or weaknesses
- **state:** express major points concisely, without using examples or details
- **summarize:** see *state*
- **trace:** similar to *narrate*; describe the chronology of an event to reveal its meaning

PERSUASIVE

In a persuasive, or argument, essay, you choose one idea and show why it is more legitimate or worthy than another. Your purpose is not to merely show your side, but convince your reader why it is best. In order to convince effectively, you must base your argument on reasoning and logic. The most important strategy for the persuasive essay is to choose the side that has the best, or most, evidence. If you believe in that side, your argument will most likely be even stronger (although you don't have to believe in it to write a good essay).

An important component of a persuasive essay is the inclusion of other points of view. They are presented in order to be refuted or weakened, thereby strengthening the case for your side. However, it is important to use reasoning and understanding to refute them. If you don't sound fair, or simply present emotional reasons why your side is best, you have weakened your argument. You must show that your idea is most legitimate in part because other ideas are weak or incorrect.

Key verbs that will help you identify a call to write a persuasive essay include:

- **criticize:** express your judgment about the strengths and weaknesses of your topic, and draw conclusions
- **evaluate:** assess the topic based on its strengths and weaknesses, drawing conclusions
- **justify:** defend or uphold your position on the topic, using convincing evidence
- **prove:** confirm or verify that something is real or true using evidence, examples, and sound reasoning

▶ PARTS OF THE TIMED ESSAY

When you have just 25 (or 45, or 60) minutes to write an essay, there is no time to waste on innovative structure. You must address the topic in a clear, well-organized fashion, using examples and details to make your point. The best way to accomplish those goals is to stick to a traditional format. Aim for an introduction, at least two to three body paragraphs, and a concluding paragraph. By writing within such a format, your ideas will be easily available to your reader (the person scoring your essay), and you will have more time to develop and substantiate them.

INTRODUCTION

The most important part of your introduction is a clear thesis statement that refers directly to the topic. Get to the point, because the real meat of your essay, where you can deliver the greatest impact to the reader, is in the body. Stating your thesis quickly and clearly means avoiding disclaimers such as "I'm not sure, but . . ." and "This may not be right . . ." Such disclaimers are a waste of time, and could prejudice your reader against your writing. No matter how strong your argument becomes in later paragraphs, that initial poor impression could stick with him or her. In addition, do not attempt to create the kind of elegant introduction that is possible to write when you have an unlimited amount of time. A confident, direct approach is best.

But direct does not mean trite. Relying on overused words and phrases to help make your point is the most common way to weaken your introduction. Compare "In today's society people don't practice good manners often enough" with "Good manners are an essential part of a civil society." The problem with the first sentence is the first three words. "In today's society" is a clichéd opening, whereas the second sentence makes its point directly, without any overused language. Review the section on Informal and Overused Language in Chapter 3 for more ideas on how to keep your word choice fresh.

BODY

In the body of your essay, you develop and illustrate the points you wish to make. It is where you add the interesting details and examples that support your thesis and make your essay stand out. Depending on the time you have to write, the body of your essay may be between two and seven paragraphs, or more. No matter how long the essay, though, remember the following advice:

- Include only information that pertains to your topic (do not go off on tangents).
- Illustrate or explain each point with appropriate details. Some essays may call for personal experiences, while others may require historical examples. Don't simply state that something is true, prove it.
- Organize your essay with multiple paragraphs.
- Use transition words like "first," "next," and "then" (see below for more useful transition words).
- Qualify your answers for accuracy. If you can't remember an exact date, approximate—"late eighteenth century" is better than 1789 if 1789 is incorrect. If you want to quote someone, but forget their exact words, paraphrase— "Thoreau noted that solitude was a great friend" is better than misquoting "I never found the companion that was so companionable as solitude."
- Take all the time you can to fully develop your ideas. If you stop writing too soon, it may be because you haven't explained yourself completely, or backed up your assertions with examples.

Transition Words

These are useful when moving from paragraph to paragraph, or point to point. Transition words help the reader follow your thoughts.

though	next
despite	another
on the contrary	in addition
nevertheless	moreover
on the other hand	conversely
similarly	yet
however	because
consequently	therefore
for this reason	as a result
after	afterwards, after this
subsequently	then

first, second, third   finally

simultaneously   it follows that

CONCLUSION

Your concluding paragraph (or statement in shorter essays) can simply restate your thesis and the points you made in the body of your essay. A restatement, summary, or conclusion can effectively reinforce these points, but remember to reword them and keep the conclusion fresh. You should not repeat your introduction, or use phrases such as "I wrote about," or "This essay was about."

If you have the time, end with something more interesting. A speculative conclusion refers to a future possibility or prediction, such as "perhaps years from now . . . " If you wrote about a problem, try a conclusion that offers a solution. If you have a fitting quotation, use it to conclude your essay. The person quoted does not have to be famous, but the quote should help you to make your point. For example, "My third grade teacher put it best . . . " These types of conclusions can leave your reader with a better overall impression of your work (although be aware that you can't overcome a weak essay with a clever conclusion).

GREAT QUESTION

"What if I come up with a great new idea when writing my conclusion?"

ANSWER

In order to use the idea, you must be able to revise your thesis statement to include it, or at least hint at it. You don't want to turn in an essay that shows you didn't come up with anything interesting until the final paragraph. A revision of your introduction can make it appear as though you had the great new idea before you even began writing.

Conclusion Checklist

✔ Do not contradict anything you said earlier in the essay.

✔ Be clear and concise.

✔ Do not introduce new information.

✔ Maintain the tone you used in the rest of your essay (review "Appropriate Levels of Formality" in Chapter 3).

✔ Do not repeat your introduction.

✔ Do not use clichéd sayings or phrases ("You can't judge a book by its cover," "In conclusion," "As I stated above").

✔ Do not apologize for anything (especially lack of time).

▶ PREPARING TO WRITE A TIMED ESSAY

As noted in the opening section of this chapter, the first step in preparing to take any essay exam is to get as much information about the exam as possible. Check the resources at the end of this book for information about your exam, and research it on the Internet. Once you have familiarized yourself with the basics, such as how long you will have to write the essay, what the topics might be, and how the essay will be graded, you can begin to prepare more thoroughly.

UNDERSTANDING YOUR TOPIC

This advice might seem obvious, but it aims to correct one of the most common mistakes made on essay exams: spend time understanding the types of topics you may encounter. Remember that your score depends in large part on how well you address the topic. But how can you prepare, if you don't know what the topic will be? Preparation materials, both in print and on the Internet, are available for many types of essay exams. If they include sample topics, familiarize yourself with them. If they simply tell you the types of topics (for instance, prompts for persuasive essays), you can find examples to study in print and on the Internet. Two great resources are *501 Writing Prompts* (LearningExpress, 2003), and school district websites (use the search term "writing prompts" on a search engine such as www.google.com).

When reading through sample topics, make a note if you understand what each one is asking you to write about. The best way to determine whether you understand the topics is to put them in your own words, and then compare yours with the originals. Are they nearly the same in meaning? If you have trouble with this exercise, go back to your list of topics. Circle the verbs (key words) in each one that tell you what to do. These are the same key words you will look for during the exam (see pages 87–89 for lists and explanations of the most common key words for both expository and persuasive essays). When you understand each topic's key words, you can more easily write the type of essay it requires.

If your essay exam includes a choice of topics, preparation should include practice with different ones, such as those that require an expository essay, and those that require a persuasive one. You might even simply outline essays that respond to the various topics. Put your work aside for a day or two, and come back to evaluate your responses. Which topic or type of topic do you write best on? Which is easiest for you? If you go into the essay exam with this knowledge, it will be much easier to choose a topic, saving you valuable time and helping to ensure you will do your best work.

THE BEST WAY TO ACHIEVE A HIGH SCORE

The scorers of every type of timed essay agree on one significant point: you must support your essay with details, examples, and evidence. They will strengthen your argument, and will make your writing come alive. Common advice for essay exam takers is to include at least one sentence in each paragraph that begins with the words, "For example." Compare these paragraphs:

High school seniors should be allowed open campuses, on which they can arrive in time for their first class, leave during free periods, and come back to school for their other classes. There is no reason to treat high school seniors like children by making them stay in school all day when they don't have classes to attend all day. Seniors can handle the extra responsibility.

High school seniors should be allowed open campuses, on which they can arrive in time for their first class, leave during free periods, and come back to school for their other classes. Seniors are given freedom and responsibility in many other areas of their lives; for example, the ability to drive a car. Seniors are also permitted to vote, and to prepare for their futures through the college admissions process or vocational training.

The first example uses generalizations and unsubstantiated claims ("no reason to treat them . . . ", "can handle the extra responsibility"), which weaken the argument. The second uses evidence, such as the responsibility of driving and voting, to make the case for open campuses. Remember to back up what you say with evidence, details, and other types of examples.

BUDGETING YOUR TIME

During your preparation, familiarize yourself with the timing of your exam. Whether you have 25 minutes, or an hour, you should spend time on three distinct tasks: planning, writing, and revising. The writing stage will take the longest, and, for essays that do not hold grammatical and spelling mistakes against you, the revising stage will be the shortest. But every essay should include all three.

Planning

The subject of prewriting was covered in Chapter 1, where six strategies are explained. Review this material, and decide, based on a few practice essays, which one works best for you. Knowing exactly what you will do when you begin the exam will not only help you save time, but it will also take some of the pressure off, too. Some exit exams (such as Indiana's Graduation Qualifying Exam) judge your prewriting notes, outlines, and other graphic organizers, making it even more important to have a strategy that you know you do well chosen ahead of time. Even if you are taking the SAT, and have just 25 minutes for your essay, spend the first three to five minutes planning.

Your planning time, no matter the prewriting strategy you use, should involve the formation of a thesis statement and three or four main points. Any supporting evidence for or examples of those points should be included. Once you begin planning, do not be tempted to switch topics, which will waste valuable writing time. Allow a few minutes to think through the topic. You may cross off main points that don't work, or add a new one or two as you go.

Writing

Using your planning notes as a guide, write your essay using paragraphs to separate your major points. Do not go off on tangents, but adhere to your plan. If you come up with another strong major point, use it, but don't freewrite or ramble. Avoid unnecessary words and phrases, including clichés (review the section on concise word choices in Chapter 2).

Keep your reader in mind. This person will give you a score based on how well you write and addressed the topic. Don't risk alienating or offending this person by using words and a tone that are too formal or too casual. You are trying to convince your reader that you can write well, and that what you are saying is reasonable and intelligent. If you alienate, confuse, or offend the reader, your essay score will suffer.

Revising

Some timed exams penalize for grammar, spelling, punctuation, and other errors in mechanics. All exams take off points for incomplete answers and failure to address the topic. Leave some time to go over your work and correct or improve any errors. Be prepared to spend between two to five minutes re-reading your essay. Check for the following do's and don'ts:

Do:

- Provide details, examples, and supporting evidence in each paragraph.
- Use paragraph breaks to help the reader see your main points.
- Transition smoothly from one idea to the next.

Don't:

- Forget to correct mistakes in grammar, spelling, and punctuation (if your exam lowers your score for such mistakes).
- Miss the opportunity to complete thoughts and phrases that could leave your reader guessing.
- Leave in rambling thoughts that are off the topic.

▶ WRITING PRACTICE ESSAYS

Put all of the information covered in this chapter to use by taking at least one practice exam. Arm yourself with a few topics, paper, pen, and a timer, and write an essay. The timer will help you to see how well you do under pressure, and how well you budgeted your time. When evaluating your practice essay, ask yourself:

- Did I finish the essay?
- Did I spend an appropriate amount of time planning and revising?
- Is the essay well-organized?
- Were there many errors in mechanics?
- Did I use examples to support my argument?
- Is the topic addressed directly and thoroughly?
- How could it be improved?

HINTS FOR TAKING THE EXAM

- ◆ Get a good night's sleep and eat a good meal before the exam.
- ◆ Bring all required items (such as writing instruments, identification, and/or a receipt).
- ◆ If there is a choice, read through the topics quickly to find the one you will write best on. Don't change your mind after making your selection.
- ◆ Underline the key words in your topic.
- ◆ Write legibly. You won't get points for neatness, but if they can't read it, they can't score it.
- ◆ Double space your essay to make it easier to read, and allow room to make corrections and additions if necessary.
- ◆ Wear a watch, and make a plan for budgeting your time.

▶ FOR YOUR REVIEW

Use what you learned in this chapter to make a checklist for studying for and taking your exam.

- Research your exam, determining how much time you will be given to write, sample topics, and what readers will be looking for.
- Understand the difference between expository and persuasive essays, and be able to locate key words that determine which kind the topic calls for.

- Be able to use each part of the essay to your best advantage, writing a strong introduction, an organized and substantiated body, and a conclusion that pulls it all together.
- Practice outlining sample topics using a variety of graphic organizers. Which one works best?
- Budget your time well, allowing at least a few minutes for planning and revising.
- Understand the topics or types of topics you will encounter.
- Practice taking a timed exam and evaluate your essay critically.
- Practice, practice, practice!

Sample Essay Prompts and Essays

In Chapters 1–7, you learned how to approach many kinds of timed and untimed essays. From prewriting and organization to editing and proofreading, each step in the process was examined. But what does it look like when all the steps are put together? In this chapter, you will get to see real prompts and real essays. Not all of the essays are top-scoring essays, but all of them are followed by an evaluation of what made the essay good, or what made the essay weak. Use these comments to reflect on what someone might write in response to one of your essays.

▶ UNTIMED ESSAY PROMPTS

UNTIMED PROMPT 1

Evaluate a significant experience, achievement, risk you have taken, or ethical dilemma you have faced, and its impact on you.

> *Sunday. As the bus bumps along through the muggy heat of July, I find it hard to be proud. Although I have just played great soccer in the Eastern*

Regional Tournament and am on my way to Regional Camp to compete with sixty other girls for positions on the East Coast Select Team, I feel tremendously nervous and inferior. Yet when I call my parents that night and learn that my grandmother is in the hospital, I realize that this week of competition is going to be much more challenging emotionally than physically.

Wednesday. I haven't been playing very well; I'm on the reserve team and my chances for advancement are slim. There is only one person who can improve my mood: my mother. Somehow she always knows just what to say. That night I call to tell her about my day and let her cheer me up. Instead, she tells me that my grandmother's situation is worse. The news hits me like a physical blow. My mind starts reeling with thoughts of my grandmother: the way she would pour her coffee into water glasses if it wasn't scalding hot, her soft, all-encompassing bear hugs, her smiling voice over the phone. The thought of this plump, joyful woman I love so much lying in a sterile hospital bed is too painful to think about, so I lose myself in a fantasy novel.

Thursday morning. Now I'm really playing poorly; my mind is with my grandmother, not my soccer ball. I look up across the field—and see my mother walking slowly toward me. I know. She's there to bring me to visit my grandmother, maybe for the last time.

Thursday afternoon. The hospital visit is eerie. My grandmother looks as if she is just barely alive, willing herself to take one more breath. I talk to her about camp, about how good the other players are, and how my game hasn't been my best. She doesn't reply, but I know she hears me. She loves that I play soccer, always telling me how lucky I am to be on a team of girls, and basking in my tales of games won and lost. My mother wants me to stay home and visit the hospital again tomorrow. I'm not sure.

Friday, a little after 11:00 A.M. After much debate, I have decided to return to the Regional Camp for the last game. I know my grandmother wants me to finish what I have started. I also feel I have an obligation to myself to follow through: I have worked so hard and so long to get to this point that I would be letting myself down if I didn't grasp my last opportunity to be selected. The coaches put me on the advanced team, and I block out all thoughts of my grandmother and play my heart out—for fifteen minutes. The game ends. Regional Camp is over, and I haven't made the team. This is the first time someone has told me I'm not good enough at soccer and it hurts.

EVALUATION

The writer of this essay detailed her involvement with soccer in a number of places on her college application, from a description of activities, to a recommendation from her coach, to a list of awards. She knew her essay shouldn't be simply another explanation of her successes on the soccer field. Instead, she combined the experience of trying out for a regional soccer team with the death of her grandmother. The result is a unique piece that tells the reader more about the writer, and displays her ability to convey her feelings and experiences effectively through the written word.

Why does this essay work? It follows much of the advice given in Chapter 6. For instance, look back to the list of qualities colleges are looking for (page 71). Of the nine qualities, only two are not included (intellectual ability and academic achievement). Next, review the tips on pages 77–78 for avoiding the most common essay blunders. Note how this essay, while it ends with a dying grandmother and failure to make the team, avoids negativity. The writer is honest about her emotions, and comes across as a strong person who, while hurt by the experiences she describes, has the strength and inner resources to keep moving forward. The piece is original, deeply personal, confident without being pompous, and set in the recent past. It is a fine example of a great essay.

UNTIMED PROMPT 2

Describe a character in fiction, an historical figure, or a creative work (as in art, music, science, etc.) that has had an influence on you.

I vividly remember the time I first heard the poem "The Dash." I was still a boy, 8th grade, and I was in an elementary school gym having basketball practice with my traveling team. Practice was almost over so, as you can imagine, my teammates and I were a little anxious to leave. We lost focus. My Coach, Dave Thomas, huddled us up at center court, and told us to take a seat. Being 8th graders, we moaned and complained under our breath about having to stay an extra couple minutes. Coach Thomas pulled out a piece of paper from his back pocket and unfolded it. The gym immediately turned quiet, we knew he had something to say. He began to read us this poem, an unusual thing for a coach to do at a basketball practice. I was listening very closely to each line. The words struck home deep down in my heart. I could feel what the writer was communicating. I was changed by that poem; my attitude and philosophy would never be the same.

The poem called "The Dash" was written by Notre Dame football player Alton Maiden. The poem is about the dash in-between the date of birth and the date of death on a gravestone. Maiden wrote, "People may forget your birth and death, but they will never forget your dash." The dash represents people's lives, what they did in their lifetime. This poem made me think about what I am doing with my dash, and what others will be left to think about my dash. It has helped me become the person I am today. I have always tried to do the right thing, and give my best in whatever I am doing. A dash without regrets as to one's efforts can hardly be a disappointment.

My dash contains music. Through music I express my thoughts and emotions.

I enjoyed playing and listening to all styles of music. In school I play drums in concert band, and also played drums and piano in a highly regarded Jazz program. Although I took piano lessons as a child, I never really enjoyed practicing and quit when I was in middle school. When I reached high school I found interest in the piano again. I taught myself how to play the music I loved and worked very hard to become a good piano player. While I enjoy playing in school, I thrive on playing outside of school. I write my own songs and lyrics and that's where I truly expressed myself. I spend more time sitting over my keyboard and recording on my computer than anything else I do. Music is something that will be with me forever, whether I am playing or listening, and I know that it's a huge part of my dash.

As high school ends and I am looking at colleges I want to make sure I continue filling my dash and State University will help in my pursuit for a strong dash. The satisfaction of facing the challenges a top notch school like State University has to offer will inspire me to keep working my hardest. State University will continue shaping me into a better person with its wide varieties of learning experiences.

My dash is something that I hold close to my heart because I know that it's the only thing I will really care about in the end. It won't matter how many points I scored, money I made, songs I recorded, or the grade point average I achieved. The experiences I've had in this life and what I got out of them is what really matters. I hope others will think of me as a hard, determined worker who always tries to do the right thing. I know that as long as I put forth my best effort in whatever I am doing, the dash will take care of itself.

EVALUATION

Referring again to the list on pages 77–78, this essay commits a serious essay blunder that weakens it considerably. It contains numerous clichés (and you might argue the subject in general is unoriginal). For example, phrases such as "struck home deep down in my heart," "helped me become the person I am today," "a top notch school," and "won't matter how many points I scored, money I made, songs I recorded, or the grade point average I achieved" are overused and stale. In addition, the writer did not carefully proofread his essay. The third paragraph carelessly shifts from present to past tense a number of times. Paragraph four begins with a run-on sentence, and there are numerous punctuation errors throughout the essay.

UNTIMED PROMPT 3

As part of a communications project and to get ready for the future, you attend a workshop called The Power of Language in the Workplace. Here, you listen to a speech given by Joseph Brown, CEO of a financial services company, about the effects of language. You think about the messages you learned by listening to this speech, and you use that information to write an essay that discusses how appropriate language is important, not only in the workplace, but in everyday life.

Write an essay in which you discuss the importance of using appropriate language in the workplace and in everyday life.

Guidelines:

Tell your audience what they need to know about using appropriate language in the workplace and in all aspects of daily life.

Use specific, accurate, and relevant information from the speech to support your discussion.

According to Joseph Brown, CEO of a prominent financial services company, language is a powerful force that can be used as a means toward great success or great destruction. In his speech, Brown told a personal story that helped him realize the power of language. Once he approached a coworker who was feeling ill with a comment about her health. He had not meant to be offensive, but his choice of words and his tone insulted her. He had to spend a great deal of time apologizing to the coworker and explaining that he did not mean to be rude. This incident caused Brown to begin observing and assessing his own language use and that of others.

Brown came to the conclusion that many people use language in a careless way. He mentioned a person in his office who frightened all of his staff members by being loud. The manager felt powerful when he used a loud, authoritative voice. His workers were afraid to interact with him. Unfortunately, this made for a very unproductive work environment because people were afraid to ask the manager questions. This meant that the workers would sometimes have to complete tasks even when they were unsure of the instructions. Rather than subject themselves to the manager's loudness, the workers attempted to do their work on their own and hoped for the best outcome.

Although Brown experienced this type of power play at work, it happens in everyday situations. Teachers may use loudness as a way to control their classes. People in social situations may use their volume to dominate the conversation. In both these instances the power of language is used incorrectly and may possibly be damaging to the listeners. Students tend to have less respect for teachers who yell at them, and therefore have difficulty learning from them. People who feel threatened in social situations tend to withdraw and this could lead to emotional difficulties.

Again, this advice is useful in aspects of life other than work situations. Even in our homes, politeness should be the norm. Siblings would probably argue less if they practiced politeness routinely. When the inevitable conflict did arise in a family, it would be more efficient and healthy if all the members "fought fair" with honesty rather than sarcasm.

At the language seminar, Brown also learned that it is a poor communication skill to combine positive and negative statements into one sentence.

According to Brown's communication experts, statements like, "This was a great report, but there are mistakes in it" are taboo. The positive part sets the listener up for a compliment and makes him or her feel good, but the negative part comes like an unexpected slap in the face. A better way to handle these situations is to point out specifically that which is good about someone's work and that which needs improvement.

Brown noticed that once people were better at using words, they were also better at doing their work. There were fewer arguments; there was less confusion, and work was done more quickly and at a higher level of quality. According to Brown, this has helped to make his company successful. The power of language is something we should all take into consideration every time we open our mouths to speak.

EVALUATION

This essay is fully developed with a broad range of information and student commentary. Specific details from the speech are accurately and appropriately given throughout. The main idea of the essay is clear: Language has the power to build up and destroy; good communication skills seek to build up, and are important in all aspects of life.

There is a logical order, with a clear introduction, a well-developed body, and a strong conclusion. The writer's use of language is sophisticated, particularly in his or her use of vocabulary ("refined," "prominent," "taboo"), which is intelligent without sounding "thesaurized." Varied sentence structure is also an indication of a sure grasp of writing skills. There are essentially no errors in grammar, punctuation, capitalization, or spelling even when the writer used sophisticated language.

UNTIMED PROMPT 4

Write a critical essay in which you discuss two works of literature you have read from the particular perspective of the statement that is provided for you below. In your essay, provide a valid interpretation of the statement, agree or disagree with the statement as you have interpreted it, and support your opinion using specific references to appropriate literary elements from the two works.

> "To be a writer, one has to tell the truth, and one has to tell the hardest truth that is available to one. One has to tell one's own truth."
> —Gordon Lish

Guidelines:

Provide a valid interpretation of the quotation that clearly establishes the criteria for analysis. Indicate whether you agree or disagree with the statement as you have interpreted it.

Choose two works you have read that you believe best support your opinion.

Use the criteria suggested to analyze the works you have chosen.

Avoid plot summary. Instead, use specific references to appropriate literary elements (for example: theme, characterization, setting, point of view) to develop your analysis.

Gordon Lish says that writers must tell the truth, even if it's hard to do. I think he's right. Stories that tell the truth like that are very powerful. I can think of two books that I read that do what Mr. Lish says. They are <u>Angela's Ashes</u> by Frank McCourt and <u>I Know Why the Caged Bird Sings</u> by Maya Angelu.

For example, if Maya Angelou didn't tell all the truth about her life, we wouldn't know about all the stuff that happened to her when she was growing up. We wouldn't understand how difficult her life was or how she survived. We wouldn't know how she turned out to be such a strong person. Like when she describes running away and living in the junkyard. That must have been a really tough experience and difficult for her to talk about. But she also tells us what she learned from that experience. Whatever she was feeling, she described it in her story. She stuck to the truth so we could see how hard it was to grow up a young black girl in the south.

We read <u>Angela's Ashes,</u> too. That story, by Frank McCourt, showed us how tough it was to grow up poor in Ireland. I never imagined being so poor! He didn't even have shoes to wear to walk to school in the winter, and to make it worse the others made fun of him for it. His dad was never around and when he was, he was drunk. And worst of all, they were always hungry. He had to steal food and stole money to escape to America. But I don't blame him. It must have been hard to admit doing these bad things and to relive all the pain in his life. If I had it that bad, I'd want to forget my past. But he told his story for us so we could appreciate what we have.

EVALUATION

This essay begins by interpreting the statement and by establishing a controlling idea. Although the interpretation is simplistic, the writer states that he agrees with Lish and then discusses two autobiographies. He doesn't identify the specific genre, but just calls them "stories." The writer offers specific details from both texts and names both authors, though he misspells Angelou's name twice.

The style of this essay is too informal, with the writer interrupting the analysis of *Angela's Ashes* twice to express his personal feelings. A statement such as "I never imagined being so poor" does not belong in a critical essay. The organization of the piece is logical and there is substantive discussion of each text in terms of the main idea, but it lacks a strong conclusion that clearly connects both texts to the quotation. The sentence structure and vocabulary are also unsophisticated, though the writing is clear and correct throughout.

UNTIMED PROMPT 5

Describe your future career plans. What experiences and influences have helped you to chose this path?

I am haunted by the question that plagues many upcoming graduates . . . what will I study in college? Many of my friends and family members assumed I would study education and become a teacher. After all, throughout my life I had always worked with children. Every summer from eighth grade through high school, I worked as a camp counselor or a summer school teacher's aide. I embraced every chance I had to be with children, and they in turn responded to my enthusiasm, energy, and the love of learning I shared with them. My interest in working with young people came naturally—I remembered how fun it was to be five years old, proud of what I could read aloud, enchanted by my newfound abilities to create sentences and stories on paper, and so utterly fulfilled by counting to 100.

Throughout high school, I have worked as a tutor at a Community Day School. I worked with underserved first through third graders. I helped create lesson plans and designed educational activities to boost students' basic reading, writing, mathematics, and creative problem-solving skills. My favorite part of the week was "Mail Time." I created a fictional character—an elf named Mijo who lived in the room in which we met—to whom the children could write short, secret notes. It was both an exercise of their newly acquired and budding writing skills, and also an outlet for problems they needed to get off their chest. Through their notes, I also learned more about what they were going through. Once a week, the children would get individual notes in return from Mijo, with words of encouragement, little observances about their progress, or short anecdotes about rough times Mijo had in the past that mirrored the students' own experiences. Mijo even had his own signature notepaper and instead of signing his name, he drew a picture of himself. It was fun to get to know the children and to understand their worlds a little bit better; it's amazing what children will confide in an elf that they won't tell adults! As I got to know the students better, I was able to see what they needed to help them learn and grow.

When I was in elementary school, I always remember looking up to my teachers, and wanting to be in their position. This summer I will be working as a teacher's aide in an after-school program. Since my class already has a reputation for bad behavior, one of my goals is for the students to understand more about their community—other teachers, each other, themselves, and me—so that they become more aware of their own values and how their actions affect the world around them. I also want my students to be exposed to a variety of learning encounters so that they understand how their own complex environments affect their experiences, and how these experiences, in turn, affect their lives. Although I know the students will still have their difficult moments, I hope they will become much more compassionate and learn to consider how their words and actions affect their peers.

I have discovered that, for me, the challenge of eventually becoming a teacher is also the lure: that as the world changes, new questions, issues, ideas, and problems must be negotiated in the classroom. Students should have the opportunity to interact with and react to what they are learning in a way that is meaningful to them, and I want to be an active participant in this process. However, I think that in order to help them be actively involved in their own learning process, I need to formalize my knowledge and build a greater understanding of how kids learn, understand more about the relative strengths and weaknesses of different educational systems, and learn about philosophies of education in a program that addresses these issues. I want to know <u>how</u> students learn, <u>what</u> motivates an individual to learn, and most importantly <u>how I can contribute</u> to improving educational systems in my own community. I want to better understand the strengths and weaknesses of our educational systems so that I can foster and support a love of learning in young people and their teachers. Additionally, I want to see the results of my work—I want to have direct contact with the learners I am serving.

EVALUATION

This essay is written to the prompt, and also takes it a step further. The writer not only describes what led her to want to be a teacher, but ends by explaining why she believes it is the right choice, and what she needs to do to prepare herself for it. The last paragraph helps the reader understand the clarity with which she made her decision.

The essay shows a good grasp of the rules of written English. There are few, if any, mistakes in mechanics, grammar, or spelling. Her word choices ("social dynamics," "creative problem-solving," "learning encounters") are sophisticated without being stiff or pompous. One suggested improvement would be greater variety in sentence structure—most of her sentences are long and complex.

▶ TIMED ESSAY PROMPTS AND SAMPLES

TIMED PROMPT 1

You have probably heard the expression, if at first you don't succeed, try, try again. What is your view on continuing to try and possibly failing before succeeding? Plan and write an essay in which you develop your perspective on this issue. Support your position with examples from your experiences, your studies, and your reading.

There are many factors involved in achieving success. But what if countless failures end with a poor result? It is not failures themselves that lead to success, but rather a combination of natural ability, persistence, and even luck.

When I started competitive swimming, at age seven, I had some natural ability. Swimming came easily to me. When shown the correct techniques for strokes, turns, and starts, I was able to employ them much quicker than many of my teammates. In fact, within a few months, I was swimming faster than some kids who were on the team for a few years. They had "failed" many times in the meets they swam in, but it didn't seem to help them understand the techniques or to come up with better strategies. I "failed" just a few times that first year, but my times were better. My natural ability helped me to achieve more in comparison with their numerous failures.

Persistence has also been a factor in my success. For the past eight years, I have attended practice at least three days a week, with a short break between each of two seasons. I swim at least 300 days a year. This persistence has allowed me to improve both technique and speed. In comparison, those who don't continue to practice frequently and find ways to swim better and faster don't make the times I do. On my old team, we practiced for a hour and a half, three days a week, forty weeks a year. On my new team, practice is five days a week for two hours, and we have just four weeks off a year. This new practice schedule has helped me to take seconds off every time, and my new team as a whole performs better than the old one.

Luck is also a factor in success. I once won a regional meet because my competitor, who was one hundredth of a second ahead, made an error and was disqualified. Another time, a competitor was sick on the day of the meet and didn't swim his best time (which would have beaten me). My successes at those meets involved, at least in part, luck.

So failure is just one part of success. The more important factors are natural ability, persistence, and luck.

EVALUATION

This essay succeeds on a number of levels. First, it takes a stand on the prompt and adheres to it throughout. Evidence and pertinent examples support the position. Second, it is well-organized. The five-paragraph structure allows the writer to explore his three chosen subjects, while maintaining a clear focus. This allows the reader to follow him easily. Third, there are very few grammar, usage, or mechanics errors. And fourth, the vocabulary is appropriate and varied. The author could have improved the concluding paragraph, which mostly restated the introduction.

TIMED PROMPT 2

Many parents give children a weekly or monthly allowance regardless of their behavior because they believe an allowance teaches children to be financially responsible. Other parents only give children an allowance as a reward for completing chores or when they have behaved properly. Explain what you think parents should do and why.

> Should parents pay children for doing chores is a good question. My parents paid me, and my brothers and sister. I never liked doing chores, but getting an allowance each week (if I did my chores) made it not so bad. In fact, sometimes I did extra (like reorganizing the pantry) to get some extra money for something I really wanted.
>
> I think having my allowance depend on my doing chores made me understand what it's like to work. In the "Real World," you don't get paid if you don't do your work. That's how it was in our house.
>
> I also learned that it's hard work to keep a house going, I learned to appreciate all the hard work my mom and dad use to do. In addition, I learned how to save money. I would set aside my allowance to save up for something I wanted, like a new CD player or outfit.
>
> In my opinion, parents should give an allowance for doing chores, but it shouldn't be too much. Children should know that they need to help no matter what. Too much money I think would make him or her feel like their hired help or something. Contrarily, too little money can make him or her feel like their help isn't worth anything to his or her parents. So finding the right amount is important.
>
> In conclusion, giving children an allowance for doing household chores is a good idea. Children learn to work for their money and save what they earn.

EVALUATION

This essay satisfies the requirements of the writing prompt in an abbreviated manner, giving only brief examples and developing ideas inconsistently. It has a general focus, there is an obvious attempt at organization, and ideas are presented in a logical progression. However, there is an uneven control of mechanics, and sentence structure is lacking in variety. Word choice is not formal enough ("made it not so bad," "hired help or something," "contrarily") and negatively affects the quality of the essay.

TIMED PROMPT 3

A few decades ago, many families had half a dozen or more children. Nowadays, more and more families are choosing to have only one or two children. Are smaller families better than larger ones? Why or why not? State your position and support it with specific reasons and examples.

I grew up in a large family—I am the oldest of six—and I have many wonderful memories from my childhood. I am very close to most of my siblings and I treasure my relationships with them. But when I have my own family someday, it won't be as big as the one I grew up in. As much as my large family was full of love, and as much as I learned about sharing, giving, and patience, I think having too many kids puts too much pressure on the parents, both in terms of time and money, and on the oldest children.

When I think back on my childhood, I remember playing with my siblings or grandparents. I don't remember spending a whole lot of time with my mother and father. They were always around, but they were always busy. My mother was always cooking, cleaning, nursing, changing a diaper, shopping, or taking someone to baseball practice, and my father was always working. He needed overtime whenever he could get it, and weekends were always full of projects around the house.

Money was also a constant worry for my family. With so many children, our budget was always tight. Back-to-school shopping was always a stressful time; we all wanted the latest fashions, but we could only get a few things. My younger siblings lived in hand-me-downs. We shopped at bargain stores and often got clothes that we didn't really like because they were on sale. Our house always needed repairs, and there was never enough money to keep up.

Another problem with large families is that the older siblings always end up being babysitters. Like it or not (and most of the time I didn't like it), I had to watch my younger brothers and sisters. At age six, I could change a diaper like a pro. I was getting my brothers and sisters dressed, giving them breakfast, helping them get ready for bed.

I don't want to give the impression that I didn't have a happy childhood. I most definitely did; I was loved as much as my parents could love me, and I had wonderful fun with my brothers and sisters. But I always wanted a little more time with Mom and Dad, and I often resented having so much responsibility. I wished my mom wasn't always so tired and my dad didn't have to work so much. Because I want to be there more for my kids, because I want them to be kids throughout their childhood, I plan to have a much smaller family.

EVALUATION

This essay is another example of how the five-paragraph essay works well for timed writing. There is a clear and logical explanation of ideas, and each main point is explored in its own paragraph. The requirements of the writing prompt are met in a creative and original manner, while the thesis remains obvious. Evidence and examples are used well to support the ideas, and transitional words and sentences guide the reader through the piece. The essay demonstrates a sense of audience by using effective vocabulary, varied sentence structure, and fluid, sophisticated language that is essentially without errors.

TIMED PROMPT 4

Describe the purposes of the Internet. Include various viewpoints, including that of users and providers.

In today's world, the first place people turn to when there is a question to be answered, information to be located, or people to be contacted, is often the Internet. The Internet has supplanted the traditional encyclopedia as well as a number of other sources of service and information. We can make reservations, plan vacations, play interactive games, learn a language, listen to music or radio programs, read the newspaper, and find out about a medical condition, without coming face to face with another person. There is no limit to the subject matter you can research on the Internet. The Internet allows you to remain at your computer and shop no matter what you wish to purchase. And if you are looking for a bargain or an unusual item, you can go to a popular auction site and either sell or buy.

But if you do wish to speak directly to a person, there are chat rooms. On practically any given topic, groups of people converse with each other. They may be giving opinions about a perfect travel itinerary, a book, or even a political party. But perhaps the widest use of the Internet involves directly writing to a person by sending e-mail messages to friends and associates. It is possible to communicate instantly with anyone, anywhere, as long as there is an Internet connection. In addition to verbal messages, digital pictures may be transmitted on the Internet.

Unfortunately, there are individuals who misuse the opportunities possible on the Internet. They are less than honest, disguise their identity, bilk people in financial scams, and entice unsuspecting people, including children, into giving them personal information. They steal people's identities and use their credit and good names to make purchases, apply for loans, and steal assets.

Of course, the Internet providers, such as AOL, hope to make a profit, and there is usually a monthly fee for the hookup. To increase the profits, the providers sell advertising, which may pop up on the subscriber's screen and require the user to stop and respond, either positively or negatively, to the ads.

When you consider that you can hear a concert, read a book, visit a museum and view its contents, visit the websites of numerous individuals and organizations, play a game with one or more people, and pay your bills, you will realize that the uses of the Internet are too vast for a short list. Most would agree that much has been added to peoples' lives by connecting them to the Internet, and that we probably cannot anticipate what new purposes will be explored in the future.

EVALUATION

This essay satisfies the requirements of the writing prompt, providing a look at the uses of the Internet by users (both good and bad) and providers. It is well-organized and easy to follow because of paragraph breaks and transitional words and phrases. The vocabulary is sophisticated, which elevates this essay. There are almost no errors in grammar, usage, or mechanics.

TIMED PROMPT 5

Personification is the technique wherein a non-human character is given human thoughts, feelings, and dialogue. Illustrate how this technique is used in your favorite novel or short story.

> Personification is the technique where the author gives non-human characters human thoughts, speech, and feelings. This is used well by Rudyard Kipling in his short story "Rikki-Tikki-Tavi."
>
> Without personification, the main character, who is a mongoose, would not be able to express his feelings. The story would need a narrator, like the kind you see on television's Wild Discovery. Some of those documentaries show animals in the wild, while a narrator tells the audience why the animals behave certain ways. With personification, a non-fictional event can be fictionalized.
>
> For example, a mongoose's natural enemy in the wild is the cobra. In "Rikki-Tikki-Tavi," the mongoose is the hero, while the cobra is the villain. Both animals have conversations with other animals and the reader can see what they are thinking about. Rikki-Tikki is nervous to fight the cobras, but doesn't show it when he starts to battle. I like how the author lets the story unfold through personification.
>
> Although Rikki can't talk with his human family, he behaves like a family pet. When the cobras plot to kill the family, Rikki defends them by killing the snakes. This story follows the common theme of good versus evil. Without personification, the story would not be so enjoyable.

EVALUATION

The writer of this essay makes some good points about personification (it allows the characters to express their feelings, helps the story unfold, and makes it more enjoyable), and uses examples from the Kipling story throughout. It is also organized, discussing three main points, and transitioning well between them. However, it could be improved through better variety of sentence structure and greater development of ideas.

Note: For more information about resources to help you write a successful essay, read the Resources at the end of this book.

Resources

Many print and online references were mentioned throughout *How to Write Great Essays*. Here, you will find more specific sources of information, including online help with text anxiety and many of the best grammar books in print.

▶ ESSAY INFORMATION

SAT
Online
- www.collegeboard.com—information from the creator of the SAT

Print
- Because the SAT essay was given for the first time in 2004, be certain you use only the latest editions of SAT preparation and information books.

GED

Online

- www.gedonline.org—literacy's site on how to prepare for the GED essay.

Print

- *GED Exam Success in Only 6 Steps* (New York: LearningExpress, 2003).

REGENTS

Online

- www.gsu.edu/~wwwrtp/—State of Georgia Regent's Site, with sample essay test form, list of topics, and scoring information
- Search for specific information on your state's test using your state name and "Regents essay" as search terms.

COLLEGE APPLICATION

Online

- www.collegelink.com—This site's services include college and scholarship searches, test preparation, electronic college applications, and advice on paying for college. You can order either hard copies or Portable Document Format (PDF) applications.
- www.xap.com—Almost 600 applications, scholarship and college searches, career information, and a high school planner are found here. No general information entry; each application must be filled out individually. Xap.com also runs 29 mentor sites, most state-based, which also provide online applications, as well as a confidential way to communicate with a college in which you may be interested. You may also transfer data from your applications directly to the FAFSA (Free Application for Federal Student Aid) on the WEB financial aid application.

Print

- Starkey, Lauren. *Goof-Proof College Admissions Essays* (New York: Learning-Express, 2003).

▶ DEALING WITH TEST ANXIETY

Online

- www.utexas.edu/student/utlc/handouts/1305.html—*How to Keep Calm During Tests*, from the University of Texas at Austin's Learning Center.
- www.sas.calpoly.edu/asc/ssl/tests.panic.tips.html—*Combating Test Panic* from California Polytechnic State University Study Skills Library.

Print

- *Secrets of Taking Any Test* (New York: LearningExpress, 1997).
- *10 Secrets to Acing Any High School Test* (New York: LearningExpress, 2003).

▶ WRITING RESOURCES

Online

- *www.bartleby.com*—without a doubt, the best online reference site. It has a searchable database of reference guides, encyclopedias, and much more. Just some of the works you will find here include *The American Heritage Dictionary of the English Language*, Fowler's *Modern English Usage*, *The Elements of Style*, and *The American Heritage Book of English Usage*.
- *http://webster.commnet.edu/grammar/*—this guide to grammar and writing, maintained by Professor Charles Darling of Capital Community College, in Hartford, Connecticut, is a comprehensive site with a particularly useful "ask grammar" service.
- *www.askoxford.com*—site has sections on classic errors and helpful hints, better writing, and ask the experts. You can sign up for "word of the day" e-mails, or chat with others about language questions.

Print

- *Writing Skills Success in 20 Minutes a Day* (New York: LearningExpress, 2001).

▶ SPELLING RESOURCES

Online

- *www.dictionary.com*—this site provides a useful online dictionary (with thesaurus). You can sign up for "word of the day" e-mails to help expand your vocabulary.
- *www.funbrain.com/spell*—this site is designed for young people with a Spell Check spelling game.

- *www.m-w.com*—the Merriam Webster Online site has a number of interesting features that will make you forget you are trying to improve your spelling! Check out the Word for the Wise section (www.m-w.com/wftw/wftw.htm) for fun facts about words.
- *www.randomhouse.com/words/*—here you will find crossword puzzles, quizzes, dictionaries, and other fun stuff all in one site.
- *www.spellingbee.com/index.shtml*—the Scripps Howard National Spelling Bee site contains "Carolyn's Corner" with weekly tips and information on spelling.
- *www.spellweb.com*—this site will help you to pick the correct spelling of two versions of a word or phrase.

Print

- *Vocabulary and Spelling Success in 20 Minutes a Day, 3rd Edition* (New York: LearningExpress, 2002).
- Devine, Felice. *Goof-Proof Spelling* (New York: LearningExpress, 2003).
- *1,001 Vocabulary and Spelling Questions, 2nd Edition* (New York: Learning-Express, 2003).
- Agnes, Michael. *Webster's New World Pocket Misspeller's Dictionary* (New York: Hungry Minds, 1997).

▶ GRAMMAR RESOURCES

Online

- *http://babel.uoregon.edu/yamada/guides/esl.html*—University of Oregon, Yamada Language Center website.
- *www.protrainco.com/info/grammar.htm*—*Good Grammar, Good Style Pages* by The Professional Training Company.
- *www.englishgrammar101.com*—this site offers several English grammar tutorials.
- *www.dailygrammar.com*—this site offers daily e-mail messages with a grammar lesson five days of the week and a quiz on the sixth day.
- *www.grammarbook.com*—the popular *Blue Book of Grammar and Punctuation* online, with simple explanations of grammar and punctuation pitfalls, and separate exercises and answer keys.

Print

- Devine, Felice. *Goof-Proof Grammar* (New York: LearningExpress, 2003).
- *501 Grammar and Writing Questions* (New York: LearningExpress, 1999).
- *Grammar Essentials*, 2nd edition (New York: LearningExpress, 2000).
- Straus, Jane. *The Blue Book of Grammar and Punctuation*, 7th edition (Mill Valley: Jane Straus, 2001).